CHRIST AND THE COSMOS

Professor E.H. Andrews

 EVANGELICAL PRESS

EVANGELICAL PRESS
16/18 High Street, Welwyn, Hertfordshire, AL6 9EQ, England.

First published 1986

Chapter 2 was formerly published under the title *Is Evolution Scientific?*,
Evangelical Press, 1979.
Chapter 4 was formerly published as a chapter in *The Bible Under Attack*,
Evangelical Press, 1978.

Unless otherwise stated, Bible quotations are from the New American Standard
Version, © The Lockman Foundation, 1973.

Andrews, E.H.
    Christ and the cosmos.
    1. Evolution – Religious aspects – Christianity
    I. Title
    261.5   BT712

    ISBN 0-85234-220-9

Typesetting by Tradeset Photosetting, Welwyn Garden City, Hertfordshire.
Printed by The Bath Press, Avon

Contents

Preface

This book is a sequel to an earlier volume, *God, Science and Evolution*. This dealt with the options available to us in the search for truth about man's origin. Expanding upon the creationist option, it explored the concept of miracles and demonstrated the rationality of a miraculous creation. The alternative of theistic evolution was examined and found to contradict biblical teaching at several crucial points.

Like its predecessor, the present work is a collection of lectures and essays which originated independently. Three of the chapters are based closely on previously published material. Chapter 2 was first published in 1977 as an illustrated booklet and went through several printings in that format. Chapter 4 is an edited version of a lecture given at the 1977 Conference of the British Evangelical Council and was published in the record of that conference which had the collective title of *The Bible under Attack*. Chapter 6 is based on the first of the annual 'Biblical Creation Lectures' sponsored by the Biblical Creation Society, delivered at Westminster Chapel in 1983. The message of all these chapters is still highly relevant in the creation/evolution debate.

Each chapter therefore stands on its own, but nevertheless contributes to a single overall theme. The thread that runs through all and imparts a measure of unity to the whole is the biblical view of the cosmos. This view, or paradigm, stands out in stark yet glorious contrast to the evolutionary scenario that is almost universally taught today.

The opening chapter provides some necessary groundwork by clarifying the relationship between faith and reason. This is important because much of what I have to say in later chapters turns on the contrast between human science and biblical revelation.

The Christian is one who believes in revelation as a valid, superior and, indeed, essential source of knowledge. Since this knowledge is 'accessed' by faith, it is vital that we understand the nature of faith as the friend, not the enemy, of reason.

Chapters 2 and 3 address themselves to the nature of evolutionary theory, but do so from complementary viewpoints. The first of these chapters examines evolution as a scientific theory. We subject its scientific credentials to close scrutiny and show that they are open to serious question. In chapter 3 we pursue this examination from a philosophical standpoint, by considering science, evolution and biblical teaching as paradigms or 'thought frameworks'. This helps to demonstrate that there are important differences between science and evolution at the philosophical level and introduces our next topic, which is whether there can possibly be any reconciliation between evolutionary and biblical world-views.

The major preoccupation of the next two chapters is this very question: can evolution and the teaching of Scripture be synthesized? There are many who claim that they can. The conflict between creationism and evolution, they assert, is the totally unnecessary product of misguided literalism on the part of some Christians. Two means are advocated to effect a reconciliation of evolution and the Bible. The first, sometimes described as 'neo-evangelicalism', makes the radical proposal that the Bible may err in matters of scientific and historical fact, while remaining reliable in its spiritual teaching. Thus, they say, Scripture has no quarrel with scientific theories of origins, because it does not pretend to speak authoritatively on such matters.

This is, of course, familiar ground to liberal theology, but it is new to evangelicals and is rejected firmly by Bible-believing Christians who understand fully what is being implied. However, there is a different approach which does not involve a rejection of biblical inerrancy, namely, theistic evolution. Chapter 5 examines theistic evolution to see whether its claim to retain a high view of Scripture is, in fact, substantiated. We see that the evolutionary and biblical paradigms both claim to embrace the whole of reality and therefore cannot both be true.

What, then, is the biblical world-view which is to take precedence over the theories of men? This is the subject of our two final chapters. Here we find it necessary to caution Christians against the careless espousal of a 'scientific creationism' that is devoid of biblical content. All creationism is not biblical. The biblical concept of creation is marked out by its Christocentricity. That is, Jesus Christ is central to all biblical teaching concerning creation. This is true whether we consider creation *ex nihilo*, the sustaining providence of God, or the purpose and destiny of the physical cosmos. Christ is all and in all.

Without this Christ-centred view of creation there is no true understanding of the cosmos. Theories of origins that neglect the role of Christ are all equally false, whether they be called creationism or evolution or by any other name.

Edgar Andrews
Welwyn, 1986

1.
Faith and reason

At first sight, our opening chapter appears to have nothing to say about evolution. However, the topic it addresses is important as an introduction to our examination of evolution because it is always implicit in any debate between creationists and their opponents. Creationists are accused of abandoning rational thought in order to maintain their faith in the biblical account of origins. This accusation is made, almost as a reflex action, whenever biblical teaching is used to deny the validity of evolutionary concepts. It is also levelled, however, when creationists advance scientific evidence for their position. In this case they are accused, not only of irrational behaviour, but also of dishonesty, for their antagonists claim that scientific creationism is merely a cover for religious beliefs.

It seems necessary, therefore, to ask whether faith really is irrational, as is often supposed. What is the relationship between faith and reason? Does the Christian believer have to abandon objective and scientific thought processes in order to maintain his belief in the Bible? These questions form the subject of this opening chapter. In it we shall see that faith and reason can never be opposed since they are quite different in kind. They operate on different levels and complement rather than oppose each other.

Intellectual suicide?

Some years ago the respected vice-chancellor of a well-known British university became so worried about the spread of Bible-based Christianity among his students that he made a public pronouncement on the subject. To believe the Bible, he claimed, was to commit intellectual suicide. In speaking like this he was only re-

peating a common fallacy, namely that faith is irrational, or opposed to reason. How can a rational person believe that the man
Jesus of Nazareth rose from the dead? How can an intelligent man
accept that Jesus was God incarnate? How can a scientifically
trained mind believe in miracles? How can an enlightened person
agree to 'medieval' notions of heaven and hell? Perhaps the good
vice-chancellor was right.

Or perhaps he wasn't. This was not, after all, the first time that
those who believe had been accused of irrationality or even mad-
ness. The Bible itself records similar reactions from the intelligent-
sia of its day. The apostle Paul was defending himself before the
Roman consul Porcius Festus, who listened in silence until Paul
referred to the resurrection of Christ. At this point Festus could
contain himself no longer, but interrupted with a loud cry of de-
rision: 'Paul, you are out of your mind! Your great learning is driving you mad' (Acts 26:24). The prisoner, however, was quite ac-
customed to such reactions and replied calmly, 'I am not out of
my mind, most excellent Festus, but I utter words of sober truth.'
Then turning to King Agrippa, an authority on Jewish affairs who
was sitting by, Paul continued, 'The king knows about these matters . . . for this has not been done in a corner.' Agrippa avoided
the challenge. He knew indeed that the body of the crucified Jesus
had vanished in strange circumstances and without explanation,
and that no one had been able to refute the claim that he had risen
from the dead.

The Greek philosophers of Athens, where Paul preached before
the court of the Areopagites, responded in a similar manner. The
book of Acts records that 'When they heard of the resurrection of
the dead, some began to sneer' (Acts 17:32). Some others, however, were not so ready to dismiss these claims and said, 'We shall
hear you again concerning this.' More significantly, we read, a
few 'believed', including a man called Dionysius, a member of the
Areopagite court.

Now this is the point of interest: although most of these
philosophers rejected the idea of the resurrection, one at least was
convinced. And this has always been the pattern throughout history as well as in Bible times. The savants and intellectual leaders
of the day have generally rejected the claims of Scripture, but
there have always been among them a few equally learned individuals who were convinced.

Paul records this interesting phenomenon in 1 Corinthians

1:23, 24: 'We preach Christ crucified, to the Jews a stumbling block, and to Gentiles foolishness, but to those who are the called, both Jews and Greeks, Christ [is] the power of God and the wisdom of God.' Those who believe are usually in a minority: 'For consider your calling, brethren, that there were not many wise according to the flesh' (1 Cor. 1:26). But *some* wise men, *some* Jews, *some* Greeks are called by God and become men of faith!

The pages of history record a long succession of princes, scholars, philosophers, teachers and scientists who, despite the scepticism of their peers and colleagues, embraced the Bible's testimony as true. What is more, we generally find that a scholar or a scientist is just as likely to evidence this faith as a labourer or a production-line worker. That is, if five in a hundred scholars are believers at some point in history, it is likely that five in a hundred manual workers are also believers. The scholarship or scientific training or intellectual power of an individual does not appear to make him more or less capable of faith.

What is reason?

Before we continue to look at the relationship of faith to reason, it will be wise to make sure we understand what reason is.

In normal conversation we tend to use words like 'reason', 'wisdom,' 'understanding,' 'rationality' and 'intelligence' to mean more or less the same thing. There is nothing wrong with this usage, but there are times when we need to be a little more precise. This is the case now, for we need to distinguish between 'reason' as *a capacity for logical thought* and 'understanding' as *the views arrived at*, or the conclusion drawn, as a result of exercising reason. Let us try to clarify this distinction by looking at some of these words.

Intelligence can be defined as 'the capacity to learn from our experiences'. Naturally, it involves the ability to observe and to record, or remember, those experiences. It also requires the ability to communicate, for otherwise we would never be able to demmonstrate whether anything had been learned or not. Animals share with man these abilities and are thus properly said to possess intelligence. Reason, however, is a higher faculty and animals can only be said to display it in the most limited sense, if at all. Reason, we said earlier, is the capacity for logical thought. What does this mean? An example will probably help.

Suppose I say to myself, 'Today is Wednesday. Wednesday is early-closing day in my local village. Therefore the village shops will be closed this afternoon.' That is an example of logical or rational thinking. I have taken two facts ('Today is Wednesday' and 'Wednesday is early-closing day') and joined them together to draw a logical conclusion or deduction ('The shops will be closed'). Note that the conclusion is not 'true' in any absolute sense. Some shops, for example, may not observe the general rule and may open in spite of its being early-closing day. Again, if this happens to be the week before a long public holiday, such as Christmas or Easter, the shops may make an exception and open their doors in expectation of increased trade. So my deduction may prove to be false, at least in part. But it remains logical or rational because there is a high probability of its being correct.

Suppose now that I indulge in another train of thought: 'Today is Wednesday. Last Wednesday, and the Wednesday before that, it rained. Therefore it will rain today.' We all recognize this as an illogical or irrational conclusion, because the probability of its being true is no greater than the random probability of rain falling at any time. Once again notice that it is not a matter of truth or error. It may, after all, rain before the day is out! It is a question of the likelihood of the thing proposed. In this case my train of thought suggests that it is more *likely* to rain today than yesterday or tomorrow. There lies the irrationality or unreason of the conclusion.

Reason, therefore, is the capacity for logical thought, and logic is judged by the intrinsic likelihood of the conclusion drawn.

Reason not the same as understanding

Wisdom (or understanding) is really quite different from reason, for it represents not so much the *capacity* for logical thought as the *conclusions arrived at* by such thought. The conclusions from an in-numerable succession of thoughts accumulate in our minds to provide both a store of 'wisdom' and a current 'understanding' of the world around us. Day by day we add to that store of wisdom and, in subtle ways, modify and revise our understanding.

To illustrate this we might represent reason as the technique of an artist – his ability to imagine, compose and execute a work of art. As he puts that technique to work, an actual picture emerges

on the canvas. The painting itself represents wisdom or understanding, namely something accumulated or built up by the exercise of reason (pictured by technique). But to produce a painting
requires *more* than the ability to wield a brush or mingle colours. It
also calls for some external stimulus or input, namely a suitably
inspiring scene, model or subject. We can represent the full
sequence by a diagram as follows:

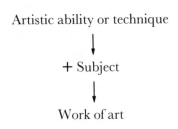

Similarly, for reason to give rise to understanding or wisdom it
has to have something to work upon, an appropriate 'input'. And
this input comes, of course, from our five senses, i.e. from observation of the world around us. We can call this input from our
senses 'sense-data' and parallel the artistic illustration as follows:

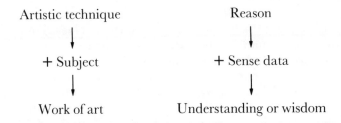

The important point about all this can now be made: reason
and understanding are two different things. Human understanding, or natural wisdom, results when reason works on the information provided by our senses. This understanding excludes any
true knowledge of God and the spiritual realm, simply because
that realm is not penetrated by the five senses, but only by faith. If
faith is absent, the religious element of our understanding consists
only of superstition as we attempt to interpret the evidence of our
physical senses in religious or spiritual terms.

What is at fault, therefore, in the natural state of man is not so
much his reason, (although that too is affected by sin) as his lack

of ability to discern or 'see' the things of God. Because this input is
lacking, no amount of reasoning can produce a corresponding understanding of spiritual truth. Consequently his understanding is
deficient and his wisdom dangerously misinformed. It is as if a
machine (representing reason) designed to manufacture car
bodies (representing the product, understanding) is fed with
cardboard sheets instead of steel. Because the input is wrong or in-
adequate, the product is equally inadequate, even though the
machine itself may be in good working order.

The antagonism of which the Bible speaks, therefore, lies not
between faith and reason, but between the natural understanding
and the understanding of faith; between human wisdom and the
wisdom of God. Thus, to use again our diagrammatic illustration:

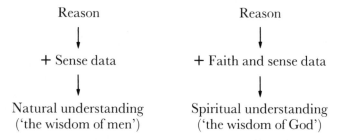

This diagram helps us to see two further things. Firstly, the
right-hand column does not just have faith on the second line, but
faith plus sense data. Thus the wisdom that results is a comprehensive understanding of the world and of ourselves as well as
of the things of God. It is not a wisdom limited to the spiritual
realm, but one which provides a unified world-view. This is important, because so many people separate their religious or
spiritual experience and understanding from their normal or
everyday outlook on life. Religious and secular activities, de-
cisions and insights are kept in water-tight compartments and not
allowed to influence each other. This is not the Bible's view of
spiritual understanding, for, says Paul, '*All things* are from God' (2
Cor. 5:18) and 'God causes *all things* to work together for good to
those that love God' (Rom. 8:28). The Bible does not permit a
dichotomy between the spiritual and the secular. God rules in the
kingdoms of men and nature as well as the kingdom of heaven,
and not even a sparrow dies without his express permission
(Matt. 10:29). The Bible claims, therefore, that only the man of

faith is totally aware of the world around him, in all its seen and unseen aspects. Only he, therefore, can possess a comprehensive wisdom, a balanced understanding.

Faith and reason not opposed

The second point that emerges from our diagram is that faith is analogous not to reason, but to the five senses. It provides information or knowledge about the unseen spiritual world just as sight, touch and so on, provide knowledge of the physical world around us. What I want to bring out here is that faith and reason are totally dissimilar things. They perform different functions, both in our diagram and in reality. No one would dream of suggesting that reason is somehow opposed to the senses. On the contrary, we recognize that reason *acts* upon the data provided by the senses.

If I am asleep, with my senses dormant, I am oblivious to the weather outside. But suppose I awake to the sound of lashing rain and howling wind. I see lightning flash and feel the house vibrate with rolling thunder. Then my reason immediately begins to utilize the information, the data, provided by those senses. I conclude that it would be wise to get up and shut the open window. I anticipate that any minute young children will wake up and be frightened. I decide that the garden will be too wet to dig the following morning or that I shall have to take the car to the station instead of walking as usual. My reasoning self is highly active as a result of the sense-data I have received. I rehearse the possible consequences of the storm, anticipating, planning and, if necessary, taking immediate action. So we may conclude that the senses actually serve reason. There is no opposition, no antagonism between sense and reason. In fact, one common usage regards the two words 'sense' and 'reason' as synonymous.

How, then, can it be maintained that *faith* and reason are opposed? For faith is nothing other than a 'sense' by which we have cognition of the spiritual realm.

Another way to express this same point is to say that faith and reason belong to different 'dimensions'; they are not of the same kind, and cannot therefore be opposites. If I were to tell you that 'late' is the opposite of 'short', you would accuse me of being illogical if not something worse. 'Late', you might point out, is an adjective relating to time, whereas 'short' belongs to the realm of space. Space and time are different dimensions. Only things of the same kind, belonging to the same dimension, can properly be compared or contrasted, related or opposed. Similarly, faith and reason belong to different dimensions and can no more be opposed to each other than can 'late' and 'short'.

Christians themselves are often guilty of confusion at this point. A much-loved hymn by Isaac Watts ends with the lines:

> Where reason fails with all its powers,
> There faith prevails and love adores.

These words suggest that faith is a substitute for reason in certain areas of thought and experience. They do, indeed, put faith above reason, ascribing to it the greater powers, but they also imply that faith and reason are of the same 'dimension'. This, I believe, is not the case. Faith is not to be likened either to reason, on the top line of our diagram, or to understanding, on the bottom line. It stands between them, alongside the physical senses, as a *means of access* to the unseen world around us. As reason acts upon sense data to interpret the material cosmos, so reason acts upon the data of faith to comprehend the spiritual universe and God himself: 'In him we live and move and exist' (Acts 17:28). Faith and reason, therefore, work *together* to produce understanding, just as sight and reason do in matters concerning the material world. They cannot be opposed.

Reason and faith go hand in hand

These ideas are supported by many of the biblical writers, who demonstrate that reason is fully employed in the pursuit of true religion.

Perhaps the clearest statement of this principle is found in Hebrews 11:3, which says, 'By faith we understand that the worlds were prepared by the word of God, so that what is seen was not made out of things which are visible.' The first four words are the ones we need to concentrate on, but notice first of all that the verse is indeed concerned with a theme which defies the unaided human mind. Even science, in all its modern development, still has no answer to the origin of matter ('what is seen'). Here we are told that matter and all the visible universe was created by the word of God. That is, it had a spiritual origin, along with space, time, cosmos. This is not a conclusion or understanding that could be arrived at by sense observation and reason alone. However, sense data *is* required, if only to reveal that there is a universe whose origin needs to be explained and, negatively, that no process observable today can account for what we see. Then faith comes into operation, revealing the existence of a spiritual being, God, who 'upholds all things by the word of his power'. Faith displays to reason the existence and nature of this God and reason concludes that a *creatio ex nihilo* of the visible universe is logically consistent with these things. Thus an understanding is achieved, by reason, on the basis of what faith reveals. 'By faith we understand . . .'

Consider some further examples from Scripture of the way in which reason and faith go hand in hand – inseparable lovers rather than antagonists!

> 'Come now, and let us reason together,'
> says the Lord,
> 'Though your sins are as scarlet,
> they will be as white as snow;
> Though they are red like crimson,
> They will be like wool'
>
> (Isa. 1:18)

The prophet here informs us that the basic issue of forgiveness of sins is a matter requiring a rational dialogue with God. It is by faith that we discern what is otherwise obscured from our understanding, namely that we are sinners. We have broken God's laws and commandments. Faith also reveals that God is a holy and a righteous Judge who holds us guilty for our transgressions. Reason, working with these facts revealed to faith, concludes that we are genuinely in trouble and that there is no assistance to be found outside of God himself! Thus our informed reason concludes that a frank and open confession of sin, coupled with a plea for mercy rather than for justice, will serve us best in these perilous circumstances. It is further revealed to faith that such mercy is available and so the rational dialogue continues. Thus we find Job, in his extremity of suffering, exclaiming,

> But I would speak to the Almighty
> And I desire to argue with God
>
> (Job 13:3)

Not only is reason engaged in our first approach to God, it is an essential ingredient of any real service to him. Paul pleads with the Roman Christians, 'Present your bodies a living sacrifice, holy, acceptable unto God, which is your reasonable service' (Rom. 12:1, AV). The word 'reasonable' is the Greek word *'logikos'* meaning 'logical' or 'rational'. The Christian who by faith has seen the mercy and goodness of God to him is logically bound to respond by bending all his efforts and powers to the service of his Lord.

In slightly different terms the apostle underlines the rationality of faith as he writes to the Corinthians: 'The love of Christ controls us, having concluded this, that . . . he died for all, that they who live should no longer live for themselves, but for him who died and rose again on their behalf' (2 Cor. 5:14, 15). The words used here imply the use of critical judgement as well as emotional response as we survey the responsibilities which fall upon the Christian.

Reason as the vehicle of the truth

Reason also finds its place in the presentation of the truth of God. On four occasions in Acts, the preaching of the gospel is represented as an exercise in reasoning. In Acts 17:2, for example, we read that 'According to Paul's custom,' he went into a synagogue and 'reasoned with them from the Scriptures, explaining and giving evidence that Christ had to suffer and rise again from the dead'. Not only, then, does reason work upon the facts revealed by faith, but it is also a proper vehicle for the presentation of those facts. Unless faith resides in the listener, of course, the facts so offered will be rejected as 'idle tales'. But where the hearer is vouchsafed the gift of faith, the spiritual realities presented to him are more readily assimilated if they are already cast in the mould of rational argument. This was the case with Lydia, whose heart 'the Lord opened to respond to the things spoken by Paul' (Acts 16:14). The opening of her heart refers to the gift imparted to her so that she was able to recognize the truth of the apostle's arguments and embrace them.

Faith and wisdom

Finally, let us take up the words 'wisdom' and 'understanding' to confirm by biblical testimony some of the assertions made in the course of this chapter. We have seen that wisdom is not the same thing as reason but that it represents a world-view built up by the interplay of sense-data and reason. We have further noticed that the natural understanding, based upon sense data alone, must inevitably differ from the understanding developed when faith is also present. If this is in any way a true picture, we would expect to find that there are *two* kinds of wisdom, *two* kinds of understanding, found among men. And this is exactly what we do find in Scripture.

'For it is written,' declares the apostle Paul, ' "I will destroy the wisdom of the wise, and the cleverness of the clever I will set aside" . . . Has not God made foolish the wisdom of the world? For since in the wisdom of God the world through its wisdom did not come to know God, God was well-pleased through the foolishness of the message preached to save those who believe' (1 Cor. 1:19–21). Thus Paul contrasts 'the wisdom of the world' with the 'wisdom of God'. The latter wisdom, he continues, exists not only in the mind of God, but is imparted to the believer through faith in Christ, who 'became to us wisdom'. Thus Paul, after dismissing the 'wisdom of men', hastens to add, 'Yet we do speak wisdom among those who are mature, a wisdom, however, not of this age, nor of the rulers of this age, who are passing away.' He is anxious to dispel any doubts about his position. He has not abandoned rationality or reason, but merely the natural understanding. The believer speaks from a more valid wisdom, 'the hidden wisdom, which God predestined' (1 Cor. 2:5–8). This divine wisdom, Paul explains, is hidden even from the leaders of this world, but it is taught to the humblest believer by the Spirit of God.

The Old Testament abounds with references to wisdom and once again we find a distinction between a wisdom imparted by God and a merely human wisdom which, says Isaiah 29:14, 'shall perish'. Thus we read that God filled certain Israelites 'with the spirit of wisdom' to enable them to perform particular tasks (Exod. 28:3) while, in contrast, we find Solomon bewailing the fact that 'In much wisdom there is much grief' (Eccles. 1:18). Jeremiah adds his evidence in chapter 9, verses 23 and

24: 'Thus says the Lord, ' "Let not a wise man boast of his wisdom, and let not the mighty man boast of his might, let not a rich man boast of his riches; but let him who boasts boast of this, that he understands and knows me, that I am the Lord . . ." ' Clearly, the wisdom in which man should not boast, according to the prophet, is natural wisdom, for it is put on a par with strength and riches. By contrast, however, he may properly rejoice in an understanding of God and his attributes of loving-kindness and righteousness. Perhaps no scripture puts the matter more succinctly than this.

Returning to the New Testament, we find again and again that natural wisdom is contrasted with spiritual wisdom. Some, suggests Paul, are 'wise in [their] own estimation' (Rom. 11:25; 12:16). Others only think that they are wise (1 Cor. 3:18). There are many who 'are wise according to the flesh [human nature]' (1 Cor. 1:26). There is a wisdom which is merely of speech (1 Cor. 1:17). After this same earthly wisdom the Greeks sought earnestly (1 Cor. 1:22). 'This wisdom,' asserts James, 'is not that which comes down from above' (James 3:15).

Over against such references we read that 'The wisdom from above is first pure, then peaceable, gentle, reasonable, full of mercy and good fruits, unwavering, without hypocrisy' (James 3:17). Stephen's opponents 'were unable to cope with the wisdom' with which he spoke (Acts 6:10). Paul prayed that God would give to the Ephesian Christians 'a spirit of wisdom and of revelation in the knowledge of him . . . that the eyes of your heart may be enlightened, so that you may know . . .' (Eph. 1:17,18). The apostle prays again, this time for the Colossians, asking that they 'may be filled with the knowledge of [God's] will in all spiritual wisdom and understanding'. For what purpose does he make this request? 'So that you may walk in a manner worthy of the Lord . . . bearing fruit in every good work and increasing in the knowledge of God' (Col. 1:9–11).

There is, then, a wisdom which the Bible rejects. It is the natural understanding which resides in human nature unaided and un-enlightened by the faculty of faith. But the Scriptures do not reject *reason*. Rather do they demonstrate how faith and reason work together in the renewed mind of a believer to produce a new wisdom, a wisdom which is from above.

2.
Is evolution scientific?

Having established that there is a proper place for reason in matters of belief, we next turn our attention to the nature of scientific theory. This is of great significance in the creation/evolution debate, because evolutionists claim that their view of origins is totally scientific and has been arrived at by purely scientific methods. It therefore has a validity (they argue) which can never be attained by subjective religious accounts of creation.

The purpose of this chapter is to call in question this claim to scientific respectability. Is evolution really scientific? How can we judge? We do so by first defining the nature of scientific theory and then testing evolution by the criteria we have established. We shall see that evolution is found wanting on several counts and cannot, therefore, claim to be scientific in the proper sense of that term.

Where does the problem lie?

The theory of evolution is all but universally accepted in the Western world today as an explanation of human origins. Almost everyone who thinks about these things takes it for granted that life began by a chance combination of molecules and then progressed through increasing levels of complexity till *homo sapiens* emerged. Claiming support from a variety of sciences, including chemistry, geology, botany, zoology and genetics, those who press the claims of evolution assert that the matter is 'scientifically proven as far as events not witnessed by man can ever be'.

Here and there, however, and apart from Christians who reject evolution on biblical and theological grounds, there are to be found scientists of various disciplines who recognize that many aspects of the theory offend the canons of rigorous science. They see that many of the so-called facts of evolution arise from carefully selected evidence and depend upon preconceived interpretations of the observations. They recognize that the mechanisms by which the evolution of life and biological species is said to have occurred are, at best, unproven hypotheses and, at worst, contradictions of the experimental facts.

So great, however, is the appeal of evolution as an explanation of life and human existence (avoiding as it does the concepts of creation and Creator) that the scientific objections to evolutionary theory are swept aside as deserving no attention or even suppressed as offensive to the rational, educated mind. Yet the spirit in which this is done, ironically, is not the careful spirit of scientific enquiry but the mindless arrogance of 'Evolution rules, O.K.?'

How has this situation come about? A number of different reasons can be given.

Firstly, much prejudice exists even among scientists, who are commonly imagined to view their enquiries with impersonal detachment. To *believe* in the ideas and theories to which one devotes much labour is an essentially human attribute, and it is extremely difficult for those human beings whose profession is science to accept that a cherished theory might possibly be wrong, even when all the evidence points in that direction. This is particularly true when the theory in question has led to a renaissance in one's field of study, as the theory of evolution has done for biology, transforming it from a pedestrian classification of the living world into an exciting search for evolutionary relationships and processes. The fact that decades of research have failed to provide any but the most specious and superficial answers to this search is a reality that the scientific community as a whole is not yet ready to acknowledge.

Interestingly enough, when one considers the separate scientific disciplines to which evolution appeals for its support, one finds, without exception, that they owe little to the ideas and dogmas of evolution. Still less do they depend on the theory for their scientific integrity. Admittedly, evolution may find frequent mention in certain textbooks, but removal of all such references would not detract significantly from the topic under discussion. One would imagine, for example, from the fuss that is made about the role of genetics in evolution, that the science of genetics is somehow based upon evolutionary concepts. Yet at least one leading textbook on genetics contains not a single reference to evolution, and I believe this example could be paralleled in other fields.

Evolution not a recognized science

The fact is (and here we give a second answer to the question posed above) that 'evolution' as such is not itself a recognized science. A student cannot graduate in such a subject or even, generally, take a course of university lectures in the field. There are, rather, a variety of scientific disciplines such as geology, palaeontology, zoology, botany, molecular biology and so on, including indeed physics and chemistry, in which evolutionary ideas are sometimes employed and evolution-related research occasionally conducted. Equally, however, the vast majority of scientists working in these areas never use the theory of evolution in their work or deal directly with its implications. Indeed, they may be no more informed about evolution than the intelligent layman, but, like the rest of us, accept uncritically what they are told. The result is that public pronouncements, broadcasts and writings on evolution come almost exclusively from a small number of scientists, writers and commentators who see evolution as a philosophy to be expounded rather than a science to be investigated. The ideas of evolution appear far more frequently in the popular press (scientific and national), which is not subject to the normal constraints of scientific verification and review before publication, than they do in the serious research journals of biology and related sciences. Certainly the speculations which often pass for 'proven facts' in evolutionary literature would not get past the refereeing procedures of most reputable scientific journals.

Evolution a philosophy

We must therefore recognize evolutionary theory for what it is – a philosophy (indeed, for some, a religion) and not basically a scientific discipline at all; only then shall we appreciate both its impact on our minds and attitudes and its decidedly unscientific character.

In the thinking of most people, evolution has achieved its initial objective of making redundant a belief in God. If man, along with all animate nature, is the product of this 'blind' process of evolution, then God is either non-existent or at best the manufactured product of our own social consciousness. It is ironical that the current resurgence of interest in metaphysics and the realms beyond our senses comes at a time when a belief in non-material powers has been rendered 'unnecessary' by a totally materialistic explanation of human origins!

What is conveniently forgotten by those who base their atheism on the evolutionary theory is that evolution, even if true, provides only half an answer, for evolution appeals to the operation of physical, chemical and mathematical laws to explain its processes, but remains forever silent on how these laws came to be or why they are as they are and not otherwise. Some, indeed, aware of this crucial point, have suggested that evolution is not, after all, a chance or accidental process, as popularly believed, but rather that the very nature of matter carries within it the potential and inevitability of evolution. Here then is a new mysticism which still does not answer the question, 'Why was matter so?,' but certainly appeals to the exact scientist more than does the traditional 'chance philosophy' of the evolutionist. This simply illustrates that some of the most fundamental questions posed by evolution are still unresolved, a statement that may come as a surprise to our well-conditioned minds which have so often been told the opposite.

Evolution provides comfort

Undoubtedly, however, the real answer to why the theory of evolution has gained such universal acceptance must lie within ourselves. Experience teaches us that we accept without question anything we find comfortable and resist ideas which cause us disquiet. If we receive a letter from the Inland Revenue enclosing an unexpected refund of income tax, we rejoice and ask no questions. An unexpected demand for extra tax, however, sends us scuttling indignantly to our files and records to prove that none is due! The idea of evolution is accepted without question by most of us because it relieves us of the need to believe in God. Some, of course, accept both evolution and the existence of a god, but the *kind* of god who remains is no longer the Almighty who called the worlds into being, and certainly not the God of creation and providence revealed in the Christian Scriptures. Instead he is a vague and somewhat redundant being, banished from involvement with the material world in which we live, hovering on the rim of human consciousness, a ghost of a god.

If this is the case, of course, a full refutation of the claims of evolution can only be given on a philosophical plane. It is not enough to reject the evolutionary world-view, but rather to replace it by an altogether more consistent and satisfying concept of nature which provides answers to man's spiritual as well as his scientific quests. The need for such a philosophy is indeed conceded by those, like the scientific humanists, who recognize that no purely materialistic interpretation of human existence is tolerable to a reasoning creature like man. They therefore propose to build a new religion, a 'religion without revelation', to quote Huxley, in which evolution becomes a mystical force and reason the new deity. Though they come up with the wrong answer, these people do at least recognize the essential dilemma posed if we accept a mechanistic evolution as the spring of human existence.

The biblical alternative

It is my belief that the consistent and satisfying interpretation referred to above is to be found in the Christian Scriptures, which provide an account of creation, nature, consciousness and being (both on the material and spiritual planes) as magnificent as it is complete. For centuries the best of human intellects have found this biblical world-view challenging, satisfying and stimulating, fusing as it does the material, moral and spiritual dimensions of human existence into a single grand and purposeful design. One of the founders of modern science, Isaac Newton, declared as the mainspring of his researches the discovery of those facts 'that would most work with considering men for the belief of a Deity,' and the unquestionable motive of most of the early natural philosophers was to reveal the hand of God in the natural universe.

It is not the purpose of this chapter, however, to set out the Christian 'philosophy of being'. Unfortunately the ravages of evolutionary thinking are so advanced in our present society that many are yet unprepared to consider the biblical alternative. It seems necessary, at least for some, to begin by removing some of the aura of infallibility that surrounds the theory of evolution. This is perhaps a 'destructive' activity, but we can learn a great deal which is to our benefit as a result.

Our purpose, therefore, is to examine critically the nature of genuine scientific theory and to apply the principles so established to the theory of evolution to see whether it does, in fact, pass muster as 'scientific' in the best sense of the word. It is hoped that in this way the reader will be helped to apply his or her own critical powers to the claims of evolution and thus become aware of some of its serious deficiencies. This in turn may prepare our minds to consider the alternatives to evolution.

The popularization of science

We live in an age of the popularization of science. Science is no longer an 'ivory tower' subject, practised and taught only in the remote fastness of the universities. Today science has a profound bearing on many aspects of our daily lives. There is nothing, therefore, wrong or inappropriate about the popularization of science. Indeed, it is very important that the layman should understand the basic concepts, methods and philosophies of science, just *because* science increasingly affects his everyday life. The threat of nuclear warfare hangs as a dark cloud above the head of everyone, and computers and medical advances affect our personal and private lives. Whether it be the ideologies of science which permeate society and influence the way we think, or the fact that often our very employment depends upon the success and viability of advanced technology – from whichever direction we approach this matter, science and its applications profoundly affect the ordinary man. It is therefore quite right that science should be popularized in the sense that scientific ideas, theories and knowledge should be taught in a simplified fashion so that ordinary people can grasp and understand them.

However, in any popularization of science there lies a danger. There are many dangers, in fact, and it is an area which has to be approached with great care. The dangers of the popularization of science show up best in phrases such as 'Science has shown . . .' or 'Scientists believe . . .' or 'Scientists have proved . . .' Whenever I read or hear those phrases I am immediately on the defensive, because I am reasonably sure that they will preface some statement which I, as a scientist, find unacceptable or distorted. Such expressions often constitute a kind of mental processing, calculated to improve the acceptability of some idea which is not really sound. They are used as a kind of insurance against any criticism of what is about to be said. If you can introduce a remark with 'Science has shown . . .' or 'Scientists believe . . .,' then it appears that you can say almost anything and get away with it!

The problem with the popularization of science is that things get simplified to such a level that they become untrue. Yet such over-simplifications are often put across to the man in the street as established facts without qualification. A theory may be advanced by a scientist, who then in the 'small print' and in technical terms adds, 'This theory depends upon this assumption and that assumption, and it will have to await this further result before we can be sure of it . . .' and so on. These qualifications, however, are swept away in popularization. The main idea comes through, but all the provisos that the careful scientist may have erected, like a fence, around his idea are swept away and forgotten and false ideas become current.

There can also arise more subtle and more tragic results from the popularization of science. It sometimes becomes possible for unscrupulous people to manipulate the minds of others by playing upon false, unbalanced or one-sided scientific principles (so-called) to justify racial, cultural or political abuses. It is quite appropriate therefore that even if we are not practising scientists we should consider the subject of scientific theory. We should at least put ourselves in the position where we can examine a statement made in the name of science, or a theory advanced in the name of science, and apply some critical faculty to it. We must be critical in the constructive sense, of course, but not necessarily accept as true everything we are told in the name of science.

In the following discussion of scientific theory I want to look first of all at its nature or character, secondly at its uses and thirdly at its abuses. Finally, because of the great importance and topical interest of matters concerned with origins, I want to apply some of the ideas we develop to the theory of evolution.

The nature of scientific theory

The term 'theory', in a scientific context, is frequently used in a rather broad and ill-defined way. One common use of the word is to describe anything within the body of scientific knowledge or activity which is not experimental. We speak of the experimental side of science and the theoretical. Now this is not a good enough definition for our present purpose. It has a certain validity, but, for one thing, it is a negative definition – theory is that which is *not* experiment – and a negative definition is not likely to help us very much. Secondly, it is too broad by far. Much non-experimental work is done (e.g. the mathematical manipulation of quantities) simply to change experimental data into a more usable form. Whether such 'data processing' is done by a computer or by a mathematician is immaterial. All that is done is to take the experimental data, the facts of observation, and put them into a form that is more usable and more useful for the application of true scientific theory. Much work is done in a laboratory, or in a scientific institution, which is not experimental but which I would not call theoretical in the true sense of that word. So to say that theory is that which is non-experimental is too broad a definition for our purpose.

Then, of course, many people think of scientific theory as that which is mathematical. To me this is too narrow a definition. In fact it is almost a false definition because mathematics differs from experimental science in one important respect. In experimental science we begin with the facts of observation, the data which comes to us as a result of observation. This observation may be common observation, or it may be some very careful experiment carried out in a laboratory, but it is none the less observation. But mathematics contains no aspect of observation. In mathematics we start with a set of axioms or assumptions. We assume that certain rules will govern our algebra; $X \times Y$ is going to equal $Y \times X$ for example. We do not have to make this 'commutative' assumption. In common algebra we choose to do so, but we can invent an algebra in which it does not apply. We make certain assumptions, adopt certain axioms and then work out the implications of those assumptions. The results obtained are implicit in the assumptions with which we begin. We are not introducing any new factor, but simply making *explicit* what was originally *implicit*. That is not to say that pure mathematics is of no use or interest. On the contrary it is a fascinating subject. But it is not scientific theory. It is of tremendous use in science, and especially in the realm of scientific theory, but scientific theory is not to be equated with that which is mathematical.

A definition

Having then rejected one definition which is too broad and another definition which is too narrow, what are we to understand by the word 'theory' when applied to things scientific?

The word comes directly from a Greek word '*theoreo*' which means 'I behold'; it is from the verb to 'behold' or 'perceive' and a theory is therefore something conceptual. It is something I perceive, something I comprehend, something that I behold in a conceptual sense. A theory can thus be defined as a concept which unifies and interrelates the facts of observation. A theory is an understanding, a comprehension which imposes order or meaning upon the facts of observation. As the scientist collects certain information or data, as he does experiments and makes measurements, he assembles the data in front of him. Then as he looks at these data, he sees that they are not independent or accidental results, but that they fit together in certain relationships. The facts of observation are like the pieces of a jig-saw puzzle, and the theory is the picture that emerges when you fit all the pieces together. More accurately, the picture is that which *enables* you to fit the pieces together.

I have a son who, when he was about two years old, used to turn the pieces of the jig-saw puzzle upside down and fit them together by looking at the shapes. Well, that is one way of doing it, but it gets rather complicated if you have a large number of pieces! Normally we use the picture and the colours to enable us to piece the puzzle together. This is what a theory does for the scientist. It enables him to interrelate, to bring together into some consistent whole, into some consistent story or picture, the facts of observation.

Interpreting the facts

A number of things stem from this definition of a theory, and there are three things I want to bring out here. The first is that *a theory is always to be differentiated from the facts of observation*. If a theory is that which co-ordinates or imposes unity upon the facts, the theory must be something *other* than the facts. Here are the facts of observation. They are brought together and we introduce a theory, a mental concept which helps us to relate and correlate the facts as we see them. A theory is thus concerned with the *interpretation* of facts, and is not to be equated with the facts themselves.

It is not uncommon in science for the same set of facts to be interpretable by a number of rival theories. The facts are not different; they are not usually disputed. But how are we to *interpret* them? You may have scientist 'A' who comes along and says,

'Well, this is my theory – this is my way of interpreting the facts,' and then scientist 'B' says, 'No, I don't see it in quite that way, I think, on the contrary, that it is this way and that way,' and so you have competing theories based upon exactly the same facts.

The relationship or correlation between cigarette smoking and lung cancer is a good illustration which is of current interest. Now, what are the facts? Well, the facts are that people who smoke heavily, especially if they have a long history of heavy smoking, have a very much higher chance of contracting lung cancer. This is the fact and nobody disputes it. But what about the interpretation? The accepted interpretation is that cigarette smoking *causes* lung cancer. Now let us be quite clear that this is *not* the fact. The fact of observation is that people who smoke heavily are much more likely to get lung cancer than those who do not. We take a theoretical step when we say, 'Cigarette smoking causes lung cancer.' There is a rival theory, very strongly supported by cigarette manufacturers naturally enough, which says, 'Oh, no! We accept the facts, but you have got your theory wrong. The correct theory or interpretation is that those people who smoke heavily do so because of some physiological or psychological need which also makes them prone to lung cancer. There is no causal connection between the smoking and the cancer. There is some other factor, factor 'X', which causes a man both to smoke heavily and to be prone to lung cancer.' We may smile and reject that idea, as most medical authorities do, but there are some very intelligent people who subscribe to it and no careful scientist will rule it out of court. You see there are two quite different theories based upon the same facts and both purport to explain the facts.

Theory, then, must be differentiated from the facts of observation. The facts can stay the same for centuries on end. They may be added to, new information may come along, but (providing they were carefully observed in the first instance) they are not going to change; but the interpretations of the facts, as the history of science testifies, change rather frequently!

Hypothesis or theory?
Secondly, *theory can exist on all levels of validity or precision.* There is no such thing as a 'typical' scientific theory, because this word 'theory', which I have said refers to the interpretation of facts, can exist in all degrees of certainty and sureness and all degrees of development and sophistication. We can start at one end with a

hypothesis. What is a hypothesis? A hypothesis is an idea put forward to explain certain observations. Strictly speaking, when we gather observations together, the first stage in our theoretical work is to advance a hypothesis. There is a sense in which all theories are hypotheses until they have been *subsequently* tested by specially designed experiment. We shall say more of this presently, but a hypothesis is a foundation for the development of ideas. It comes from a Greek word which means 'to put beneath', 'to lay beneath', 'to place underneath'. A hypothesis is a foundation. It is not, therefore, something flimsy and insubstantial. In fact, it is quite the opposite. It is a *substance*, a foundation, a starting-point, a premise. It is not a complete theory any more than a foundation for a building is the complete building, but just as a building needs a foundation so any theory needs a hypothesis. So at its first inception the new-born theory is a hypothesis, something proposed but ill-developed, a basic concept which enables us to develop ideas and to build a self-respecting theory upon it.

The hypothesis stands at one end of the theoretical spectrum. At the other end there is the fully developed theory which passes into the book as 'natural law'. We talk about the law of gravitation and the laws of optics. These are theories which have not only been advanced to explain facts, but which have been developed and established by subsequent experiment and by various tests. They have stood the test of time and further investigation; they become well established and they pass into the realm of scientific law. There is therefore a vast spectrum of posssibilities. If I say I have a theory, you may properly ask, 'Where in that spectrum does the theory lie? Is it a hypothesis, a starting-point, a premise on which to develop ideas? Or have you worked all the way through it, and have you come to a finished, complete, tested theory which we can call a scientific law? Or does it lie somewhere between these extremes?' That is the second point, that theory can exist on all levels of validity or precision.

There is one very real problem that we meet at this juncture. We start with a hypothesis. There is no difficulty in providing a hypothesis, but when we want to develop it into an established theory, real difficulties may emerge because some of the things we need to do, by way of experiment, to prove our hypothesis and to strengthen our theory, are for one reason or another inaccessible. Let us take the lung cancer example once again. Having put forward the hypothesis that smoking causes lung cancer, what is needed is to take a hundred individuals of all kinds (those with this mysterious factor 'X' and those without it) and put them into a prison and force them to smoke cigarettes for twenty years and then see how many get lung cancer. This would prove the point beyond any question, but obviously it cannot be done. We could perhaps simulate the experiment by using mice or rats, but nevertheless you cannot really do the experiment that you need to do to enable you to convert your hypothesis into a more established form.

This problem arises in an acute form when we try to provide theories to explain historical events like the origin of life or the development or evolution of a species. We cannot go back, we cannot go into the laboratory and do the appropriate experiment. The same problem arises in dealing with very remote events, like stellar evolution or astrophysical reactions and processes. You cannot bring them into the laboratory and do just the experiments you might like to prove your point. These are very real difficulties and it means that in certain branches of science one has to be content with theories which are barely out of the stage of the hypothesis, whereas in other branches of science, physics or chemistry perhaps, you can prove or disprove your theory very happily by going into the laboratory and doing special experiments.

Theory not reality
Thirdly, *theory is at best only a model of, or an approximation to, reality.* This goes even for theories which have become very sophisticated, highly developed and which are fully amenable to testing in the laboratory. Let us take the example of the structure of the atom. This is a subject which has been worked on, I suppose, since the time of the ancient Greeks, but effectively for something like a century. A tremendous amount of sophistication has been possible. The first of the modern concepts was that of Rutherford, who was able to show that the positive charge in the atom is concentrated in a small region of space which is called the 'nucleus'. He proposed a picture of a central nucleus surrounded by orbiting electrons, much as the planets orbit the sun. The very fact that one likens it to the solar system means that it is only a picture, a model. It is not the reality, but merely an abstraction or simplification of reality. Like any model, Rutherford's atom explained or accounted for certain facts, but not for all of them, and very soon this

model was in dire trouble because it appeared to contradict the laws of electrodynamics. Then Niels Bohr came along and said, 'The trouble is, we are trying to apply rules that may not apply on the scale of the atom. We must adopt new laws, we must introduce new rules to explain the stability of the atom.' So he proposed a more sophisticated theory, the quantum theory of the atom. The idea was further developed so that no longer did one think of a single orbiting particle, like a planet going round the sun, but of the probability of finding a certain electrical charge at a particular point in space. Now this explains other things that could not be explained on the simpler models. You see, the model is getting more and more complicated, but it is still a model. Thus, a theory is never a reality; it is always a model or a representation of reality, more or less crude.

Consider that other classical example, the nature of light. Originally men like Newton believed that light was corpuscular, consisting of particles. That idea was dislodged by the phenomenon of diffraction and it became evident that one could only explain the behaviour of light by saying that it consisted of 'waves'. Then, of course, further experiments were made and it was found that the idea of particles, the corpuscular concept, had to be reintroduced. So here is a case where the phenomenon of light was first of all viewed as corpuscular in nature, then as wave-like and then again as corpuscular. Eventually the situation has been reached in which we have to say, 'Really light is both corpuscular and wave-like.' Sometimes it behaves like a wave, sometimes it behaves like a stream of particles. Thus 'reality' can only be expressed by two quite contradictory models. The reality is more complicated than the model, and in this case so complicated that, in order to picture it at all, we have to adopt a dual model comprehending two apparently opposed concepts. Quite obviously the model corresponds only crudely with the reality which we call light.

There is therefore much in any theory that does not correspond to reality. Data must be smoothed out, interpolated and extrapolated before arriving at the theory which is a satisfactory model, for the time being, of that which one is trying to represent. But it is, in the last analysis, *only* a representation.

I have spent a great deal of time on the nature of theory and I have said three things about it: theory is to be differentiated from the facts; theory can exist on all levels of validity or precision; and theory is at best only a model of, or an approximation to, reality. We are now in a position to consider the uses and abuses of this thing we call scientific theory.

The uses of scientific theory

We now look very briefly at the uses of scientific theory. I do not want to spend a lot of time on this because to some extent it is self-evident. This section could be developed at length, but it is not the main purpose of this chapter to do so. Suffice it to say that theory is an intrinsic part of the body of scientific knowledge and of the activity that we know as science. It would be impossible to have science without theory, because without theory science would simply be a collection of data, a gathering of information and perhaps a classification of that data. Science would be a sterile, dead-end kind of activity if there were no theory. The excitement and the interest of science is, having collected the information, the data and the observations, then to be able to impose on them some meaning and some significance – to be able to say, 'I behold, I see a pattern, a picture, a meaning, a significance here.' Science, as we know it, could not exist without theory.

Understanding the universe
Science, in my view, has two functions. First of all, *it is a method which enables us to comprehend the universe in which we live*. This is really science for science's sake, for the sake of knowledge (the basic meaning of the word 'science' is 'knowledge'). It is the accumulation of knowledge, not simply as data and facts, but as an understanding or interpretation of the material world around us. It is worth noting here that many, if not all, of the early modern scientists, driven, of course, by that curiosity which is natural to the human mind, were very concerned that their understanding of the universe through science should be a God-honouring and a theistic understanding. Johann Kepler is said to have cried out, on his discovery of the three laws of planetary motion, 'O God, I am thinking thy thoughts after thee!' Now this is a point worth making. He was making discoveries, not only about the universe, but about God. He was discovering the creation, but in doing so he believed he was discovering the Creator. Sir James Jeans is supposed to have said that 'Behind the universe there is a great

mathematical Something.' We may consider that a rather in-adequate concept of the nature of God, but we see nevertheless that he is looking at the universe through the eyes of science and reasoning through to the Creator; he is making statements about the character and nature of that Creator.

Of Isaac Newton it has been said that 'Belief in God rested for him chiefly in the admirable order of the universe,' and he himself said that he practised science in order to make discoveries that would convince men that God is, and that God is glorious and that God is all-powerful. Robert Boyle published his various theological treatises to emphasize the harmony between the new scientific methods and Christian faith.

We must, I suppose, recognize that there was a basic fallacy from a theological viewpoint in what these men were doing. This is an aside, but it needs to be said. Their idea of using natural theology, the discoveries of science, to convince men of the being and character of God is not theologically tenable. It was based upon the assumption that men only had to be shown and told, in order to believe. Now we know, of course, if we are Bible students, that there is a barrier to man's understanding. In 1 Corinthians 2:14 we read that 'A natural man does not accept the things of the Spirit of God; for they are foolishness to him and he cannot under-stand them, because they are spiritually appraised.' The natural man does not have the spiritual eyesight, the spiritual capacity, the spiritual faculty to believe in God until God gives it to him as a gift of grace. These men were wrong (they were well-meaning, but they were wrong) in trying to convince others of the existence and character of God through the work of science. They had left out of account the fallen nature of man. But, nevertheless, they were trying to use scientific theory as a means of comprehending and explaining the universe in a theological sense.

Practical application of theory
The first use of science and scientific theory, then, is to com-prehend the universe around us. But, secondly, *scientific theory has a use in its application.* All engineering, all applied science, with the vast array of activity that these expressions represent and com-prehend, are concerned with the predictive use of scientific theory. This is disguised, but in a very real way we use scientific theory in a predictive sense whenever we design a structure or machine of any kind. We say, 'If I build this electric motor with this number

of turns of electric wire, it will generate this particular power at this particular voltage.' We are using the laws of science to predict what will happen if we make our machine in a certain way. This is the process of engineering design. Because the theory employed is at the well-established end of the spectrum of which I have been speaking, the electric motor does more or less what it was designed to do. Generally speaking, therefore, engineering is an illustration of the predictive use of scientific theory, and it is unnecessary to emphasize the influence of such activities upon our daily experience. No doubt, in most cases, these effects are beneficial to mankind.

The abuses of scientific theory

These then, very much in a nutshell, are the uses of scientific theory. Now let us move on to the abuses. The abuses of scientific theory arise when the nature of scientific theory, which concerned us in the first part of this chapter, is forgotten or ignored. It is generally true that abuse of anything arises when the nature of that thing is forgotten or ignored. We can therefore look at the various abuses which parallel the several statements made earlier about the nature of scientific theory.

1. Confusing theory with fact
The first abuse arises *when theory is equated to, or confused with, fact* — when the theory, which is the interpretation of facts, is confused with the facts of observation themselves. I have already laboured the point that this is what very commonly happens in the popularization of science. When you are trying to present something very simply, you can easily present the theory as something equal to the facts, rather than an interpretation of the facts. This error arises because, in presenting a simplified or popular picture, it is easy to present the theory or the concept and leave it at that. You may never get around to presenting the facts upon which the concept is based and from which that concept has been derived.

Much of my time is spent training Ph.D students and sometimes they come along to me with an idea, a theory and say, 'I can explain it all this way.' Sometimes I am rather suspicious and I say, 'Let me look at your original data.' Quite often I find that the data fail to support the theory. I may say to the student, 'You have said there is a linear relationship between X and Y, but when I look at the points on the graph I don't see a linear relationship; I see a general scatter of data.' So, by calling for the original facts, I have got underneath the theory that has been proposed and I have questioned that theory. But if I present a theory to you as popular science, I do not usually present the facts to you at all. I say, 'This is the case; there is a linear relationship,' meaning only that I have interpreted the data in that particular manner. The layman, denied access to the underlying facts, usually has no alternative but to accept the statement at its face value. Thus confusion easily arises between the facts and the theory. One man's highly publicized interpretation may become equated with reality in people's minds. I call this abuse the abuse of '*dogmatism*'; dogmatism is when a theory is presented as reality, as fact, instead of as an interpretation of facts.

2. The danger of extrapolation

The second abuse is that of *extrapolation*. That is when a theory, which may be perfectly good in one realm, is extended, without justification, into realms where it is not known to apply. We can take Newtonian mechanics as a good example here. Newtonian mechanics, the rules or laws which govern the motion of solid bodies, apply beautifully to most of the observed world. But when you try to apply Newtonian mechanics to the structure of the atom, you meet with insurmountable problems. Again, when you try to apply Newtonian mechanics to objects travelling at very high speeds, approaching the velocity of light, failure again results. The same is quite possibly true for events and objects that are extremely vast in astronomical terms. We have, then, a perfectly valid and respectable scientific theory which applies over a limited range, but if we try to extrapolate that theory and force it to apply on an atomic scale, or to things travelling close to the velocity of light, we shall be doing violence to it and our predictions will be false. So there is a danger in extrapolation, of taking a valid, established theory which applies to a narrow realm of nature and extending it into regions where its behaviour and its validity have not been established.

This is a very real and serious problem, which is frequently encountered in research work. Imagine somebody is plotting a graph. Their experiments have led them to locate three points which appear to lie on a straight line. So they draw a straight line through them and extrapolate or extend that straight line into a region of the graph where they have no experimental data. They claim that this straight-line relationship holds for the whole of the 'space' considered, but this may not be the case. For all we know, that 'straight' line may turn around upon itself and change direction as it moves into a different area of the graph. The matter can only be resolved by making further measurements.

3. The abuse of exaggeration

The third way in which theory can be abused is by *exaggeration*, that is, when the theory is accorded a status which is inappropriate to its degree of validation. I said earlier on, and spent some time in arguing the matter, that theories could exist on all levels of validity, from the hypothesis right through to the law of nature. If you take a hypothesis and endue it with the standing of a law of nature, you are abusing scientific theory. It is always important to give a theory the status, to attribute to it the validity, which is appropriate to its level of development.

4. Emotional involvement

Then fourthly, and perhaps this is the worst abuse of all, there is *subjectivism*. This arises when a theory is defended *against* the facts of observation, i.e. when a theory is maintained in spite of new facts which emerge to indicate that the theory is inadequate or false. Unfortunately, this happens all the time because scientists are human beings and they have emotions like other human beings. There is a degree, sometimes a strong degree, of emotional involvement of a scientist in his work. If a man has spent his whole life developing and building up a certain theory, he is not going to take kindly to new evidence which destroys that theory. There is a common joke among scientists, that if you have two or three results that seem to prove the thing you want to prove, you should refrain from carrying out more experiments, in case the next result *does not* agree! I had an example of this myself. We were investigating the mechanical strength of particular adhesive bonds and using a theoretical analysis to evaluate these results. Providing we used certain substrates to make the bond everything fitted beautifully with the theory and enabled us to understand the nature of the interatomic forces operating at the bonded interface. The trouble is that if you go on to use other substrates the theory does not work any more, and has to be greatly modified to encompass the 'new' results. The temptation is to stop one's thinking at the point where it works and to ignore or to dismiss the unpleasant facts which come along, sometimes later, to show that the theory is not as good as was thought in the first place. There is this conservatism, this subjectivism which makes us all want to defend our theoretical understanding of nature against any new facts that arise.

This is not the popular concept of science, of course. Science is so objective in the popular view that every piece of evidence is taken purely on its merits, but in reality this is not so. Scientists tend to select the evidence that supports their preconceived ideas. In this respect they behave like the normal human beings they really are!

5. Exploitation
There is a fifth abuse which I will mention briefly. This occurs when scientific theory is used to justify activities in the non-scientific realm, to justify political, racial, social or even tendentious educational developments. This we could call the abuse of *exploitation*.

The theory of evolution

How do these things apply to the theory of evolution? Here we can quite easily discern many of the abuses enumerated in the previous section. I cannot discuss these things at great length here, because this is really the starting-point of an entirely new debate! I just want to note the ways in which some of these abuses of scientific theory have been, and are, displayed by the theory of evolution.

1. Evolution taken for granted
First of all, of course, the theory of evolution is regarded very much as a fact, as describing events that really did happen. Commentators and the mass media present evolution in this way, often quite gratuitously. If someone on the BBC is describing a certain kind of bird in a nature programme he will often say that in the course of evolution the bird 'developed' this kind of beak, or foot, or wing – whereas you may well know, if you are a biologist, that nobody has ever studied the 'evolution' of that particular

bird. There has perhaps never been any investigation of it at all. It is just taken for granted that if a bird *has* a wing or a foot or a beak of a certain kind, it must have got it through a process of evolution. There could be no other way by which that particular result could have been reached! Thus evolution is regarded as a fact, even in cases never subjected to study. Now the facts upon which the evolutionary theory is based do not add up to anything like the theory of evolution. The facts are sparse; they are often debatable and very uncertain. Even where the facts are clear, well-displayed and easily ascertainable, they would often lead an impartial observer to conclusions which oppose the theory of evolution.

I want to illustrate this by quoting from a Frenchman, Professor Vialleton. He wrote as long ago as 1924, but nothing has happened to change the validity of what he says. 'There is then,' he writes, 'when one considers evolution in the light of the real evidence, both great doubt, and also exaggeration of its value, resulting in the idea that is very anthropomorphic, namely that everything has always begun very humbly and later has developed into very complex and lofty forms. Once again, one must say that this is not the picture presented by nature. One scarcely sees throughout the geological ages a gradual, slow multiplication of types of organization. One does not at first find a unicellular being, then simple colonies of cells, then cellenturates, etc. On the contrary, Louis Agassiz remarked a long time ago in 1859 that in the first known fossils one finds, side by side, representatives of all the great groups except the vertebrates. Which seems to prove that the living world from its origin has been composed of diverse types, perfectly distinct one from the other, which have divided among themselves the various functions of life. Evolution has not begun from forms truly simple in order to pass over into more complicated forms. The types of organization one finds (i.e. in the fossil record), have always displayed their essential character initially, from the very outset. Genuine evolution, therefore, as one ascends the geological column from the first to the last representatives of any type of organization, is trivial in sum and scarcely permits one to believe in the overweening power to effect biological transformation.'

One could multiply that kind of quotation. You see, the facts *do not* point to evolution. The facts of the fossil record, if anything, point to something other than or contrary to evolution, but because evolution is regarded as a fact, these matters are never brought out. So I believe that evolution is guilty of this error of *dogmatism*, i.e. the abuse of equating theory with fact, whereas the facts are often at variance with the theory.

2. *Evolutionists guilty of extrapolation*

Secondly, in evolution, one finds the error of *extrapolation*, and this comes out in two ways. First of all, the observable processes of mutation and natural selection, which can be observed in the laboratory – processes you can actually carry out and see happen and with which there are no real problems or difficulty – have been forced back in time to 'explain' changes of a kind that have never been observed in the laboratory – changes of a magnitude which cannot be envisaged in terms of anything that ever has been observed. I remember once, some years ago, picking up a particular edition of the *Encyclopaedia Britannica* and reading the article on evolution. I think it was by Haldane, although it was only signed by initials at the end. In the course of this very pro-evolutionary article there came a very significant statement. It was the admission that if the evolution of species has taken place as envisaged by the theory, then mutations must have occurred in the past which were both of a kind and of a magnitude never observed in the laboratory. I have never seen that quotation in any subsequent edition of the *Encyclopaedia Britannica*. Perhaps it was just too much of an admission. The theory of evolution requires the extrapolation of observable things, such as the various changes that can be wrought in the fruit fly, on which a tremendous amount of work has been done, to realms and events remote both in time and scale from the area in which the ideas have been validated. Thousands upon thousands, even millions, of generations of fruit fly have been bred and acted upon by X-rays and all kinds of means to produce mutations at a high rate, but nothing has been observed which could possibly account for even the most publicized steps in the supposed evolution of species. No changes were induced that could, by analogy, explain such 'classic' examples of claimed evolution as the giraffe growing a long neck, or the bird's feather evolving from a reptile scale.

So much for one kind of extrapolation of which the theory of evolution is guilty. The second is a more philosophical extrapolation, in which the concept of evolution is extended to the whole of nature, from biological evolution to chemical evolution (the evolution of the first living molecules by random process) back to stellar evolution and to such ideas as the continuous creation even of matter itself. The same idea takes the theory of evolution and extrapolates it forward into the future to 'control' the evolution of society and effect the development of the human species in a manner governed by man. This attempt to take evolutionary philosophy and extrapolate it to all corners of our experience and our universe is another abuse of theory and as such is fraught with danger.

3. The hypothesis of evolution

The third abuse to be seen in the theory of evolution is that of *exaggeration*. The theory of evolution really ought to be called the hypothesis of evolution, because that would describe more accurately the stage of development of the ideas which it contains. One must be sympathetic here. There are so many things that cannot be put to the test in a laboratory. It is impossible to advance this theory by retracing the steps of time and performing experiments to evolve another horse or another bird. The time scale appealed to by the theory is just not available to us and there is the special difficulty of the uniqueness of such past events. But no matter how much one may sympathize with the difficulties of establishing a hypothesis, we must face the fact that the theory of evolution has not grown, and is never likely to grow, out of the infant hypothetical form. To consider it almost a law of nature, an established fact, rather than the hypothesis that it is, is to yield to the error of exaggeration. The biologist Dobzhansky, a man who believed in evolution, wrote in *Science* in 1958, 'The occurrence of the evolution of life in the history of the earth is established about as well as events not witnessed by human observers can be.' That is the first and most important admission, that man can never test this theory because its workings can never be observed by human beings. He continues, 'The most pressing problems of evolutionary biology seem at present to belong to two groups, those concerned with the mechanics of evolution, and those dealing with the biological uniqueness of man.' Freely interpreted this surely means, 'I believe that evolution happened, but I do not know how.'

There are other abuses. There is the abuse of evolution for political ends. I do not intend to develop this idea here, but one has only to go back to the use that the Nazis made of the evolutionary concept to justify their mass murder of the Jews, to see how, if these theories get into wrong hands, they can be desperately misused. Communistic atheism is another creed which appeals to evolutionary ideas to justify its political activities.

4. *Ignoring the facts*

Finally, there is the error of *subjectivism*. This is the tendency to reject facts which do not fit the theory, instead of accepting the facts and adjusting the theory. It is as if a tailor found that the suit he had made did not fit the customer's body and wanted to alter the man instead of the suit! You must not do violence to the facts in order to fit your theory. That is an abuse of theory, yet it is frequently done in evolutionary teaching! If the facts do not agree or concur with what the evolutionist believes, then he will frequently cancel out, deny, ignore or otherwise undermine these facts. The fossil record, for example, is replete with so called 'anomalous' findings which are either left on one side or explained away by extravagant and unlikely hypotheses.

Conclusion

In this review of scientific theory I have tried to show how an understanding of its true nature and its legitimate uses can protect us against its misuse. Theory, above all, is an interpretation of the world of our experience. It represents a generally honest attempt to rationalize the kaleidoscopic procession of information gathered, moment by moment and day by day, by our various senses. Inevitably, our rationalizations are also simplifications, models of reality rather than ultimate truth. Indeed, it is one of the chief functions of theory to simplify and to bring order to the multitude of our experiences so that we may live in mental equilibrium with the world around us.

Because, however, theory is our attempt to impose rationality upon this incredible universe, it is no less prone to error than are the mental processes which give rise to it. Scientific theory partakes of the same powers and the same limitations as the men who make it! In particular it is not free from its own kinds of prejudice. Properly used, it can be a powerful servant to man in his exploration and enjoyment of the universe. Misused, it can only be the enemy of truth, whether scientific or religious. To understand its nature and its limitations is the basic wisdom which must be exercised whenever we handle scientific theory.

3.
A choice of paradigms

We have just seen that evolution does not pass muster as a truly scientific theory. We now pursue this theme and examine more closely the philosophical nature of evolution and how it differs from genuine science. In doing so, we make use of the concept of paradigms, the patterns of thought that underlie all our interpretations of experience. We trace the differences and similarities among three important conceptual frameworks, the scientific, evolutionary and biblical paradigms respectively, and ask the question: 'How far can they be reconciled?'

What is a paradigm?

The word 'paradigm' is a technical term from the realm of philosophy, but it is gradually passing over into common usage. It was introduced by the philosopher Thomas Kuhn to signify an intellectual framework, though even Kuhn himself used the word rather freely without precise definition.

Basically, a paradigm is an example or pattern and the word is used in this literal sense in reference to grammatical (e.g. verbal) structures. What Kuhn did was to extend this meaning to apply to a pattern or framework of ideas or thought. For the purpose of this chapter, therefore, we shall define the word in the following manner: A paradigm is a set of ideas, concepts or assumptions which provides a framework within which men may interpret their experiences. To give a simple example, the same experience of a thunderstorm may be interpreted by a primitive tribesman as a display of anger by the gods and by a scientist as an interplay of electrical phenomena. The experience is the same, but the interpretation is quite different, because the two observers are operating within different paradigms. The concept of electricity is missing from the tribesman's paradigm, while that of god or gods may well be absent from the scientist's. While we recognize the superiority, in this instance, of the scientist's paradigm, we must be careful not to say that one paradigm is wholly true and the other wholly false. Indeed, if pressed, the scientist would find it just as difficult to explain the ultimate nature of more 'electricity' as the tribesman would to explain 'gods'.

Our example illustrates another important point. The paradigm we adopt in the interpretation of our experiences is not entirely of our own choosing. There is a sense in which neither the scientist nor the tribesman can help seeing things the way he does. Their respective paradigms are not so much the product of rational choice as the result of their cultural setting and upbringing. Thus we all adopt paradigms to some extent unconsciously, our basic assumptions about life and the universe being moulded by the religious, political and social environment in which our minds develop.

The reason for our interest in this subject will emerge more clearly as we proceed, but we can note here that the paradigm we adopt (the framework of ideas we use to interpret the world about us and our own inner perceptions) must inevitably shape our total outlook on life or 'world-view'. Our beliefs and our behaviour are alike dictated by the basic, and often subconscious, assumptions that underlie all our attempts to make sense of life.

Many readers will have travelled to different parts of the world and will have noticed great differences between the attitudes and outlooks of different societies. These differences can often be seen within a given nation, where rural and urban attitudes, for example, may differ quite profoundly. What we are seeing in these instances are not so much racial differences as examples of different paradigms or patterns of thought. Thus money may assume an importance in urban societies which it does not have in the thinking of country dwellers, and many other more complex distinctions could be cited.

In this chapter we are going to look at a number of different paradigms adopted by people today, and especially at three of them. These are the 'scientific paradigm', the 'evolutionary paradigm' and the 'biblical paradigm' respectively. We shall also examine attempts that have been made to synthesize two or more of these paradigms into a single one with a view to reconciling apparent conflicts between them. Notice that our primitive tribesman will receive no further mention. This will remind us that the paradigms dealt with in what follows by no means cover the whole gamut of those available to man. Each of the religions practised the world over, for example, has its own separate paradigm, as does each different culture. The paradigms considered here, however, have the distinction of rising above merely cultural differences. Indeed, much of their importance lies in their ability to unite men of different cultures.

The scientific paradigm

The ideas that make up the scientific paradigm are not difficult to summarize. They are broadly as follows.

1. All events in the physical or material realm are due to the operation of the laws of nature.
2. These 'natural laws' are universal, that is, they remain unchanged throughout space and time.
3. Natural laws are established or discovered by experiment and that which cannot be so established is not part of scientific knowledge. (Note that experiment includes observation of the natural world.)
4. Theories, whether mathematical or conceptual, are scientific only if they make predictions capable of verification (or falsification) by experiment.
5. In the present state of scientific development there are many aspects of human experience that cannot be described or explained scientifically. On these matters science can make no pronouncement.

Let me make several comments at this point. The statements made above are not intended to provide a rigorous definition of 'science'. There could be much debate, for example, over the nature of scientific theory. Karl Popper's famous dictum that a theory is only scientific if it is in principle falsifiable is considered by some philosophers of science to be too narrow, and other areas of disagreement emerge as one looks more closely at these matters.

The paradigm outlined above is intended to be a general statement of the assumptions underlying modern science. Indeed, one
of the features that distinguishes a paradigm from a list of prop-
ositions or a credal statement is the fact that it is not clearly defin-
able. It is fuzzy at the edges, if you like, since it has continually to
adapt itself to new experiences. A paradigm's main function is to
provide a framework within which we may interpret experience,
but it is not wholly immune to change. If the things we experience
refuse stubbornly to fit into the paradigm we are using, the latter
has to give way under the pressure of the facts. It has to stretch to
accommodate what it cannot otherwise contain. Sometimes this
accommodation is so drastic that the paradigm itself is destroyed
and a new one established in its place, and this is essentially what
happens when a person is converted from one set of beliefs to
another.

The scientific paradigm we are considering here is that of modern science, as mentioned earlier. The science of ancient Greece,
for example, though in many ways foundational, was based on a
significantly different paradigm, in which the importance of experiment in formulating natural law went largely unrecognized.
For them, pure thought was the touchstone of scientific progress
and mathematics took pride of place over empirical science. A
similar but more subtle distinction can be drawn between
twentieth-century science and that of the earliest founders of
science as we know it.

This can be illustrated by a remark made by Isaac Newton
(1642-1727). He comments, 'When I wrote my treatise about our
system [the '*principia*'] I had an eye upon such principles as might
work with considering men for the belief of a Deity and nothing
can rejoice me more than to find it useful for that purpose.' This is
far more than a statement that Newton believed in God. It indicates, rather, that his belief in God directed his scientific en-
deavours. Newton was by no means unique in this respect, for one
of the explicit purposes of these early men of science was to demonstrate the existence and attributes of God in so far as these are
manifested in the natural order. It was their declared objective to
refute the growing rationalism of their day. Belief in God was
therefore such an integral part of these men's science that their
'scientific paradigm' would have to include the proposition that
the natural order is the work of an intelligent Creator. The
paradigm of twentieth-century science has been shorn of this

theological content and this is just as true for the scientist who believes in God as for his atheistic or agnostic colleagues.

This brings us to the fifth point listed above, namely that the scientific paradigm does not claim that science embraces all truth or even all experience. A scientist who believes in God may adopt the paradigm for the purpose of his scientific work and thinking without rejecting the possibility of miracles. These are excluded from the paradigm, but only in the sense that science has nothing to say about such events. The paradigm does not say that miracles are impossible, merely that they lie outside the realm of scientific consideration. Of course, an unbeliever may embrace the scientific paradigm as total truth, holding that nothing can occur that is not the consequence of scientific law and that there is no reality beyond the material world. This stance, however, encounters an insuperable problem, in that scientific law itself (its origin and rationality) cannot be explained within the paradigm. For, self-evidently, natural law cannot be a consequence of itself!

The whole scientific paradigm is built around the concept of natural law. Without such law science would simply not exist. Yet the paradigm has nothing to say about the source or origin of those laws and therefore does not pretend to embrace all reality. After all, the laws exist. They form part of our experience, both scientific and common. Yet the cause of their existence and the reason they take the particular form that they do are subjects that the scientific paradigm ignores.

This is not accidental, of course, since any debate about these matters is excluded by the insistence in the paradigm upon experimental verification. The origin of natural law is simply not accessible to scientific study (experiment). The laws themselves are studied, of course, but their source or reason lies beyond the material realm in which science operates. Questions regarding the origin of natural law must be categorized as religious or philosophical, not scientific. It follows that the scientific paradigm does not pretend to comprehend the whole of reality.

This is a very important point to grasp, since it is often claimed (or at least implied) that science can in principle offer 'explanations' for everything that lies within the scope of human experience. This opinion often finds its expression in the negative form, when it is suggested that science describes the real world while philosophy and religion are concerned with imaginary or unreal things. This common materialistic world-view is based upon a misunderstanding of the scientific paradigm.

Another area of human experience that is ignored by the scientific paradigm is that of morality in its widest sense. To put it simply, science can decide whether a statement is true or false, provided that the statement refers to the material world. What it cannot do is to determine whether an action or an opinion is right or wrong in a moral sense. Naturally, in the light of this dilemma, some have attempted to derive moral rules or principles from science, but this is doomed to failure because the scientific paradigm contains no elements that bear upon moral issues. The only way that such attempts can succeed is by adding moral dimensions to the paradigm itself, but if this is done the paradigm ceases to be purely scientific and the attempt is self-defeating. No one can claim that his philosophy is purely scientific in origin, for all philosophy involves presuppositions that lie outside the scientific paradigm.

We see then that the scientific paradigm, by virtue of its self-imposed limitations, applies only to a limited range of human experience and violence is done to it when people try to apply it universally. Much human experience lies beyond its capacity to comment or to guide, though its precise limits of applicability are open to debate. This matters because, to a large extent, the evolution/creation controversy turns on the question of how far the scientific paradigm can be applied to the subject of origins.

The evolutionary paradigm

Evolutionists claim that the theory of evolution is simply a branch of science and would not accept the idea that the evolutionary paradigm differs in any way from the scientific one. I would suggest, however, that there is a most important difference. This difference lies in the addition of a fresh assumption of *uniformity*.

One of the features of the scientific paradigm was the assumption that natural law is universal, unchanging in space or time. This is a principle of uniformity, of course. But the uniformity that lies at the heart of evolutionary thinking is of an altogether more radical kind.

Firstly, evolutionary uniformity holds that not only natural law, but also natural process is unchanging. In geology this is known as the 'uniformitarian principle' and can be expressed simply by the saying: 'The present is the key to the past.' Thus processes such as mountain formation, continental drift, sedimentation and so on are assumed to have occurred in the past at the same rate as they occur today. While geologists recognize that there have been 'catastrophic' events in the past history of the earth, it is supposed that they played no major part in the formation of the world as we know it. The same principle of uniformitarianism is applied in evolutionary biology. Thus mutation rates observed in the laboratory today are used to interpret past biological change.

It is important to notice the profound difference between the uniformity of natural law and the uniformity of natural process. They are quite different principles. Great non-uniformity can occur in natural processes while natural law continues to operate with complete uniformity. Thus a large increase in mutation rates may be produced if organisms are exposed to high doses of radiation, an event which may well have happened in the past due to fluctuations in the shielding effect of the earth's magnetic field. No changes in natural law are involved in such circumstances. Similarly, geologists have claimed that in the recent creation of the volcanic island of Surtsey, off Iceland, events occurred in a few weeks or even days which elsewhere would have taken thousands of years. Again no change of natural law is envisaged by such statements, but merely that the rates at which processes take place in the natural world are not fixed but are related to the magnitude of the forces which produce them. These forces may (and do) vary greatly from place to place and from time to time.

It will be seen, then, that uniformitarianism is not part of the scientific paradigm at all, but an ingredient added to permit today's observations to be extrapolated backwards into the past.

Secondly, evolution also applies the principle of uniformity in a more philosophical way. Whereas the scientific paradigm appeals to the uniformity of natural law in a pragmatic sense, the evolutionary paradigm uses it in a dogmatic sense. All scientists have to assume that the experiments conducted yesterday were subject to the same scientific laws as those to be conducted tomorrow. Experience shows this assumption to be fully justified, since repeated experiments usually give the same results after long intervals of time. From time to time, however, physicists are found speculating on the possibility of long-term 'drift' in the value of certain fundamental constants of nature, or upon the violation of such laws as the conservation of energy and matter, again on a very long time-scale. Such speculations are not considered to be scientific heresy. The scientific paradigm does not regard uniformity as a philosophical necessity, but employs it as an empirical fact within the limits of our capacity to test it. Science recognizes that the laws it formulates are imperfect representations of reality and that further research may lead to modification of those laws. By definition, therefore, no law is inviolate and the assumption of uniformity must be seen in the light of this proviso.

The emphasis in the evolutionary paradigm is different. Uniformity of both natural law and natural process becomes a guiding principle. All observations have to be interpreted in a manner consistent with this principle; all theories must conform to it. Uniformity thus becomes a philosophical straight-jacket which prohibits rational alternatives. Let me try to illustrate this.

It would be perfectly consistent with the scientific paradigm to suppose that there existed a historical discontinuity in the operation of natural law as we know it. That is, we might propose that before a certain time in history, the laws governing the natural world were different from those we know today. Of course, an atheist would protest that there is no earthly reason to introduce such an idea, since it certainly cannot be deduced from observing the present world order. A Christian, on the other hand, might well envisage such a discontinuity as marking the end of the creation period as recorded in Genesis 2:1-3. Either way, it remains true that the scientific paradigm would not deny such a discontinuity but would merely refrain from any comment on the matter since it limits itself to an era in which law is empirically unchanging.

To the evolutionary paradigm, however, the idea of a historical discontinuity is repugnant since it violates the philosophical principle of uniformity. On this paradigm there simply can be no discontinuity, because uniformity throughout all history is axiomatic. All past events, whether historical, biological, geological or cosmological, must be part of the undisturbed flow of uniform process.

Notice that this is a belief, a philosophical principle adopted before considering the facts of science or revelation. It is not a scientific deduction from the facts of observation. This is obvious, since we are discussing time-spans vastly greater than the time-scale of scientific study. It is true that uniformity is found to hold over short time-spans, but scientific method itself warns us against extrapolating results too far along any axis of variability (in this case, time). What is true of the uniformity of natural law is doubly true of the uniformity of natural process. In the latter case there is, in fact, considerable evidence in nature that past events occurred that have no counterpart today. Massive glaciations, volcanic outflows, the formation of vast fossil graveyards – all these have occurred in the past on a scale totally unknown today. To assume uniformity of natural process is an act of faith indeed.

I am quite willing to admit that the principle of uniformity has a philosophical elegance and simplicity that render it attractive. It is consistent with the short-term observations of uniformity and it minimizes the number of assumptions that have to be made concerning past events. But this makes it convenient rather than true. Any research scientist knows how often an elegant and simple theory has to be abandoned in the light of new facts which reveal unsuspected complexities in the system under investigation. Convenience has to yield to observation. The problem arises when such a principle is applied to realms where no experimental test is possible, such as the remote past. In these cases the principle of uniformity shapes our thinking instead of reflecting reality.

If uniformity is the guiding principle of the evolutionary paradigm, the concept of evolution itself is its categorical imperative. Evolution means 'unfolding' and an evolving universe is one in which uniform natural process leads to an inexorable growth in complexity and diversity. Here is another distinction between the scientific and evolutionary paradigms. The scientific world-view is committed to observation and makes no *a priori* statements about the direction or results of change. It may be that observation leads to the conclusion that all systems, left to themselves, must degrade. That is, they eventually become more uniform (less diverse or complex). This is the conclusion of the science of thermodynamics. But the scientific paradigm *derives* this concept from the observations. It does not *impose* it upon them before they are made.

The evolutionary paradigm, in contrast, does impose upon the observations a belief that all things are unfolding to reveal new and hidden potential. This is starkly illustrated by a quotation from Teilhard de Chardin: 'Human knowledge is developing exclusively under the aegis of evolution, recognized as a prime property of experimental reality. So true is this that nothing can any longer find place in our construction which does not first satisfy the conditions of a universe in the process of transformation. A Christ whose features do not adapt themselves to the requirements of a world that is evolutive in structure will tend more and more to be eliminated...'

Notice that evolutionary change is viewed not only as an 'experimental reality', but that anything that does not conform to the idea of evolution must necessarily be excluded from the evolutionist's thinking. This is an extreme statement, especially as it embraces the religious as well as the material realm, and some evolutionists would not accept it totally. It does, however, exemplify the logical conclusion to which the evolutionary paradigm would drive its adherents.

Theistic evolutionists often draw a distinction between evolution as a subject of scientific study and 'evolutionism' as a philosophical creed. This attempt to separate the wheat from the chaff is certainly honest and even helpful, but it really begs the essential question. For evolutionary studies, by their very nature, cannot content themselves with 'things as they are', but insist that today's observations be extrapolated back into the remote past in order to explain the present world order. All such extrapolations involve the prior assumption of the principle of uniformity, not as a scientific observation over a limited time-span, but as a philosophical prerequisite. Evolution and evolutionism are therefore not different in essence but only in emphasis. Evolution is just as intolerant of historical discontinuity as is evolutionism. The principle of uniformity is the philosophical imperative that lies behind them both.

The biblical paradigm

In contrast to the paradigms considered so far, which begin with man and his experience of nature, the biblical paradigm begins with God. This is not to say that God lies beyond the experience of man. If this were so there would be no biblical paradigm, for God would be unknowable! The whole message of Scripture centres in the claim that God may be known, for Jesus said, 'This is eternal life, that they may know thee, the only true God, and Jesus Christ whom thou hast sent' (John 17:3). The Bible, however, begins with the objective reality of God, rather than with God as an aspect of human experience. This is expressed perfectly in Hebrews 11:6 where we read, 'Without faith it is impossible to please [God], for he who comes to God must believe that he is, and that he is a rewarder of those who seek him.' The experience of God follows from an acceptance of his existence; his existence is not deduced from our experience.

Some will immediately dismiss this approach as 'blind faith', but this is a superficial judgement. What we actually have here is what we might call 'the hypothesis of God'. Frequently in science we advance hypotheses before there is empirical evidence to support them. The word 'hypothesis' means 'foundation', a basis for further development. The hypothesis is literally, therefore, a foundation for subsequent experiment, something that guides our thinking as we explore the matter more deeply. We may say, 'Suppose this is true,' and then proceed to work out the implications of our hypothesis and test them by experiment. The Bible invites us to proceed on the assumption that God exists and to work out and test the implications of that assumption.

There is, of course, a difference between a scientific hypothesis and the assumption that God exists, for man is by nature blind to the spiritual realities of God in a way that he is not blind to the material world. Even the first steps towards God, therefore, require that a man be endowed with spiritual sight and this is what the Bible calls faith. 'We look not at the things that are seen,' explains Paul, 'but at the things which are not seen' (2 Cor.4:18). Such faith, we are further told, is received from God as a gift (Eph.2:8).

The next ingredient in the biblical paradigm is the identification of God: he is the 'living God, who made the heaven and the earth and the sea, and all that is in them' (Acts 14:15). It is interesting to note how the apostle Paul always begins at this point when addressing those ignorant of the Old Testament. At Athens he elaborates the theme, introducing God as the one 'who made the world and all things in it' and who 'gives to all life and breath and all things' (Acts 17:24,25). Such words specify not only that God exists, but that he stands in a particular relationship to the created order, especially man himself.

One important implication of the creatorhood of God is that he himself must transcend creation. He cannot be part of that which he has brought into being. This introduces the idea of the spiritual (that is, the non-material) nature of God. 'God is spirit,' declares Christ, 'and those who worship him must worship in spirit and truth' (John 4:24). Since spirit creates matter, the spiritual realm both transcends and co-exists with the material cosmos. The physical universe exists within the matrix of the spiritual.

A third major concept in the biblical paradigm concerns the nature of man. As we have seen, man is part of God's created order, but Scripture accords him a special place in that order. For man alone, of all living creatures, was made 'in the image of God' (Gen.1:26,27). This signifies that the nature of man involves a special relationship to God, special privileges, special responsibilities and a special purpose or destiny. Any world-view which ignores the 'specialness' of man must conflict directly with the biblical paradigm.

The next aspect of the biblical paradigm follows immediately from this and concerns its moral content. Here again we find a distinction between the biblical and the scientific or evolutionary conceptual frameworks. In the biblical paradigm, morality stems from the unchanging character of God. What is 'good'? It is that which answers to the nature and will of God. What is 'evil'? It is that which conflicts with his nature and opposes his will.

Morality, of course, is a concept known to men everywhere, whether or not they are familiar with the Bible. Some claim that morality has an evolutionary origin, suggesting that where human society has been regulated by moral laws, there also has existed stability, which in turn increases viability. Thus morality has 'survival value' and is consequently encouraged by the process of natural selection as it applies to societies.

Careful observation shows, however, that this is not the way morality actually operates. Human societies always tend to become corrupt and this leads to self-destruction. Frequently in human history, however, the process of decline is arrested by a reformation of one sort or another. What produces reformation? Almost always it stems from the teaching or activity of an individual or small group of individuals standing against the accepted standards of their day. Often such reformers pay for their efforts with their lives. Reformation certainly does not have survival value for its advocates; the reverse is more likely! The source of reformation in human society can be traced therefore, not to its survival value, but to the consciences of men.

Conscience itself is a debated concept, but in the biblical

paradigm its existence and origin are not in doubt. It is a manifestation of the image of God in man. Man alone out of the whole animal kingdom shares with God the distinction of possessing a moral nature. Thus even those who know nothing of biblical revelation have 'the requirements of [God's] law... written on their hearts' (Rom.2:15, NIV).

The biblical paradigm, however, goes further than this. It classifies man as a moral being and then proceeds to show that he is also *fallen*. He not only possesses moral powers and responsibilities, but a bias towards evil and against God. This is a most important aspect of the biblical paradigm, because the 'sinnerhood' of man underlies his thinking, his behaviour and (above all) his need. With respect to his thinking, sin keeps him from knowing truth. With respect to his behaviour, sin explains man's tendency to corrupt himself and his society. With respect to his need, human sin predicates the mission and saving work of Jesus Christ. 'It is not those who are well who need a physician,' said Jesus, 'but those who are sick. I have... come to call... sinners to repentance' (Luke 5:31,32). Lacking this saving work of Christ, man lies under God's judgement and this manifests itself in several ways. Man is first of all left to reap the consequences of his own sin. Secondly his mind is darkened. Thirdly he is separated from God for ever (Rom.1:21-25; Rev.20:11-15).

The last ingredient of the biblical paradigm that we need to mention is the concept of 'revelation'. Since man in sin is incapable of arriving at truth by his own intellectual efforts, it is necessary for truth to be revealed to him by God. This revelation, states the biblical paradigm, is granted to men on an individual basis through the dual agency of Scripture and the work of God's Spirit.

It is not claimed that the Bible contains all truth, for the Scriptures themselves refer to a fulness of knowledge awaiting those who, by the grace of God, will one day be united with Christ in a glorified state. The Bible does, however, claim to contain all that is necessary for the salvation of men and their enjoyment of God in this present life. To summarize, therefore, the major themes of the biblical paradigm can be set out as follows:

1. God exists.
2. God is the Creator and Sustainer of the physical universe, while being himself transcendent of that universe (God is spirit).
3. Man is a special creation; he alone of all creatures is made in

the image of God. That is, man is a moral being, equipped with conscience and possessed of moral responsibilities.

4. Man is fallen and lies under judgement for his sin. He is incapable of attaining a knowledge of the truth without the provision and application (by God's Spirit) of revelation.

5. God's purpose and intent in revelation is to save men from sin and judgement through faith in Jesus Christ and bring them to share his glory. The very purpose of creation is bound up with this ultimate saving work of God in Christ.

Reconciling the paradigms

Is it possible to reconcile these diverse paradigms? Since each paradigm is followed by many people, it would obviously be beneficial to effect a synthesis of the scientific, evolutionary and biblical paradigms.

It is certainly possible to reconcile the scientific paradigm with either the evolutionary or the biblical world-views. The reason for this is that the scientific paradigm does not claim to be 'holistic', that is, to encompass all reality. It limits itself, as we have seen, to the material realm and passes no judgement upon matters outside its own sphere. These 'outside' matters include not only the spiritual world, but also such issues as the nature and the origin of natural law, and morality. The scientific paradigm, admittedly, excludes the spiritual realm. But so, equally, does it exclude morality. By excluding these areas of human experience it does not imply that they are unreal or unimportant, but simply that they are not amenable to scientific method.

This being so, there is no conflict between the scientific and the biblical paradigms. The latter is holistic, claiming to embrace the whole of reality, including that sub-division of reality to which the scientific paradigm addresses itself. By the introduction of miracles, for example, the Bible emphasizes the normality of natural law, for miracles can only be significant if there exists a natural order of events to be superseded or suspended when a miracle occurs. We have already noted that in the early days of modern science the orderliness and design in nature revealed by scientific study was believed to underwrite the biblical concept of a Creator.

Similarly, the scientific paradigm is consistent with the

evolutionary world-view. The reason for this is the same as for the biblical paradigm, namely that evolutionism is holistic and science is not. This is why we spent time earlier to establish that the evolutionary paradigm goes much further than the scientific and adds to the latter a number of philosophical axioms. Another way to express this is that the evolutionary paradigm is a philosophical extension of the scientific paradigm in which concepts in the material realm are held to cover all reality. Thus while science ignores the spiritual realm but does not deny its existence, the evolutionary world-view categorically excludes God by insisting that all reality is a consequence of natural process. Evolutionism denies duality (the co-existence of the material and spiritual realms) and forces all reality into a unitary system in which natural process is the new deity.

Although I say that evolutionism is an extension of the scientific paradigm, it is not a *legitimate* extrapolation, since it violates one of the essential ingredients of science, namely the need for experimental verification. The evolutionary paradigm seeks to explain in natural terms the origin of all things. Such claims can never be subject to experimental test and this is freely admitted by evolutionists. They proceed, however, on the basis that the extrapolation of natural process is justified. In what way is it justified, we might ask? On the principle that the simplest explanation is the truest (a form of 'Occam's razor'). If everything can be explained in terms of natural process and if there is no need to invoke a miraculous creation, then the need to believe in miracles is removed. God is made redundant.

The principle which 'justifies' the evolutionary paradigm is thus seen to be frankly philosophical. It is the deliberate exclusion of dualism, the appeal to a unitary world-view for its own sake or its intrinsic elegance. This might be justified if the resulting world-view *could* explain all human experience, but of course, it cannot do so. It therefore becomes necessary, in the evolutionary paradigm, to relegate all religious experience to the realm of fantasy, and all 'inexplicable' events to the realm of that which yet awaits discovery.

It is quite clear, then, that the evolutionary and biblical paradigms are mutually exclusive. Either may be reconciled with the scientific paradigm, but not with each other. This is because each of them is 'holistic', seeking to embrace the whole of reality. They cannot both be true, for they propose totally different views of God, man and nature, and both claim exclusive truth for what they teach.

4.
The Bible under attack

'With friends like these, who needs enemies?' This rueful rhetoric is apposite as we come to the subject matter of the next two chapters. In the previous chapter it was argued that no reconciliation is possible between evolution and the Bible because both claim to be holistic (i.e. total) explanations of being. In spite of this, many Christians do attempt to synthesize evolutionary and biblical thinking. Their effects are well intentioned, but fraught with danger. Biblical Christianity may have more to fear from its friends than from its enemies.

There are two quite distinct groups of people involved in these attempts at reconciliation. Firstly there are the 'neo-evangelicals', who achieve their purpose by allowing that the Bible may err in matters of history and science while remaining accurate on spiritual issues. Secondly, there are 'theistic evolutionists', who often adopt a fully conservative view of Scripture, but argue that the Bible can be interpreted in a manner consistent with the claims of evolution. Our next two chapters deal with these two approaches in turn and point to the positive alternatives available to the Bible-believing Christian.

The root of the problem

As I considered how I should approach this subject, two alternatives presented themselves to me. The first, which I have rejected, would have been to rehearse the growing case against an evolutionary interpretation of life and nature. There is a fundamental reason for taking a different approach to our subject. I believe we have to raise the level of our discussion beyond the arguments for and against evolution, important though they are. We have to deal with the root of the problem. We are faced with a philosophical problem and we shall never make progress in this particular battle while we stand around the edges of the subject simply sniping at our opponents. We have to come to the heart of the matter which, as I hope will emerge from the following pages, is not basically scientific at all, but philosophical and theological.

This more philosophical approach is necessary because unless we understand and proclaim the theological framework of our understanding of nature, of life and of creation, we shall not provide anything positive. It is all very well to be purely negative and to say evolution cannot have happened because of this and that and something else. It is quite simple to demonstrate that certain aspects of the theory of evolution are plainly incredible, but that is not sufficient. What we must do in our debate with the world around us is provide a positive alternative to evolution. It is within that larger and more positive framework that we must operate, preach and teach.

What I have to say can be considered under two headings. Firstly, the attack and secondly, the answer. Although this analysis is very simple the matters that we are dealing with are weighty indeed.

The attack

I want to suggest that the attack comes to us from four directions.

The materialistic world

First of all, it comes from a materialistic world-view. It comes from a concept of creation and all that it contains, of time and life and human history, that is materialistic. Many would say that the view to which I refer is scientific, but I would reject that submission. I believe it is materialistic rather than scientific.

What is this materialistic world-view which constitutes the first source of attack upon the biblical doctrine of creation? It is one with which we are all too familiar. In a sense it is unnecessary for me to rehearse it because it comes to us from the mass media, from popular literature, from newspapers and magazines, from radio and television. It features in our school lessons and our school books, our university courses and our university texts. It is an attempt to explain the phenomena of life and man, and indeed the entirety of nature, in terms of the operation of scientific law alone.

This materialistic world-view must begin, of course, with some origin which it cannot explain – a genesis in which the entire universe came into being in some catastrophic and unimaginable explosion – the so-called 'big bang'. According to this idea the universe as we know it now, the stars, the galaxies and the earth (as a tiny speck of dust amid this cosmic turmoil) are but the fragments and the debris of that primordial catastrophe. This account of the universe tells us how stars evolved and how they go through a life cycle in terms of billions of years. It looks back to the 'big bang' which occurred something like 6,000,000,000 years ago and concludes that the earth itself is a cinder, the result of a subsequent supernova explosion, which is perhaps four thousand five hundred million years old. This view pictures the earth cooling down gradually until some of the processes we know today began to operate. The processes of solar irradiation and lightning discharge are supposed to have produced, from small and simple molecules in the earth's atmosphere, larger organic molecules. These molecules were washed down into the seas and rivers of the earth and there they became increasingly concentrated. In this concentrated form they joined together to form larger molecules, and eventually these larger molecules separated from the aqueous medium in which they were dissolved. They became encapsulated and, in some way which even the evolutionists do not yet attempt to explain, were transformed into the first living cell. This then began to multiply and duplicate and acquire the ability to undergo genetic variation. Upon that genetic variation there operated a process of natural selection until, from that first tiny spark of life, there arose the whole order of living things and, to crown it all, man himself.

This is the world-view which (let us not deceive ourselves) the vast majority of men and women in our Western society accept today. Of course, there are features of this view which we as Christians cannot accept and I want to list those features in case we are unclear about them.

Why can we not believe this world-view? Why can we not accept this picture, this materialistic scheme, of how things came to be? Well, the first and most obvious reason is that *it leaves no place for God*. God is totally unnecessary either as a concept or as an agent within this process. It is true that many Christians claim that this world-view is essentially correct except that it leaves out the meaning and the purpose that God can provide. So they attempt to graft the idea of God on to this materialistic picture of the universe. But, as I hope we shall see, you cannot superimpose God on such a picture. There is an innate conflict, an intrinsic irreconcilability, between the concept of God and this materialistic view. If you want to build God into your view of the world, then you must *begin* with God. You cannot add him as an afterthought, because if you try to do so he becomes dispensable to anyone who does not like the idea of God. And, as we know from our understanding of Scripture, the human heart in general does not like the idea of God. Romans 1 explains this perfectly clearly. Man did not like, and does not like, to retain God in his knowledge.

We all need an interpretation of the world around us, for it is quite intolerable for a thinking creature like man to live without some answer to the 'why' of our existence. It is therefore very attractive to the human heart, in its sin, rebellion and blindness, to accept a theory of being that dispenses with God. It is no use our saying, 'Oh, no! You *must* have God to provide meaning.' They will say, 'No thank you! We can provide meaning from other sources and in other ways. We will do without God because our materialistic description and world-view is perfectly adequate.' So not only do we reject this world-view because it has no place for God; we also reject it because, secondly, *it satisfies the unregenerate human heart*. It provides for that heart a place of escape from the challenge of the concepts of creation and Creator, from the implication that there is a God who made us and to whom we are answerable.

There is a third reason why we, as Christians, must reject this view, and this is that *the Bible tells us perfectly plainly that creation is a finished work*. Creation is not an ongoing process which is still to be observed today; it is a completed work. The evolutionary view begins with the evolution of the universe, proceeds onward to the origin of life by chemical evolution and then to biological evolution. Indeed it goes on, in the minds of many people, to the concepts of directed and man-controlled evolution. The view that evolution gives us, therefore, is that of an unfinished and ongoing process. But the Bible states perfectly plainly that God saw the things which he had made and declared them not only good, but complete and perfect. We are told that on the seventh day he rested from all his labours. Creation was finished.

Now we must not allow the evolutionists to confuse us at this point. They will say, 'But we can demonstrate that evolution is going on today. We can point to this variation and that variation in this species and that species and we can show you that evolution is an active process observable today.'

What they are really pointing to is *variation*, not evolution. Now it is quite evident that the Bible teaches variation because, just to quote a single point, all the varieties of the human race – black, white, red, yellow and all the racial distinctions among men – have been caused by variation during the descent of the human race from Adam. The Bible does not say that God created half a dozen different types of human being. He created one man and one woman and from that single pair have descended all the varieties, the pygmies, the giants, the Eskimos and the Negroes, the Caucasians and so on. Thus the Bible provides for a tremendous amount of variation within a kind. (We must not fall into the trap of identifying the 'kinds' of Genesis with the scientifically defined species of today.) Of course there is variation, and when people quote such things as the industrial melanism of moths as evidence for evolution, it is nothing of the kind. It is simply an example of variation. Within the limits of that variation, natural selection may well operate. We have no quarrel with that idea. The quarrel is with the concept that all living kinds have arisen from a single original form by a process of mutation and natural selection. That is what we must reject on biblical grounds.

A fourth reason why we must reject this materialistic world-view is that *evolution works in the opposite direction to the processes that we see operating in Scripture*. Evolution is ever upward, from imperfection to perfection and from simplicity to complexity. In contrast, the Bible demonstrates a creation that was originally perfect and complete and infinitely complex, and the only direction of change is that of deterioration. There has been sin. There has been a degradation of God's original perfect creation. There has been a downward movement, not an upward movement. I find it impossible to reconcile those two opposites.

Then, fifthly, we must reject this materialistic world-view, because *there are specific conflicts with the Word of God*. People often suggest that evolution tells roughly the same story as the book of Genesis, but such a claim will not stand up to close examination. To cite one example only, Genesis makes it clear that life arose first on earth (plants), not in the sea, as evolution claims.

2. Atheistic philosophies

I have spent a considerable time on the materialistic view of nature because, in a sense, it is the most basic direction from which attack comes. The next two directions of attack I am going to deal with very briefly. The second is that of atheistic philosophies. Whether we are thinking of atheistic communism, scientifc humanism, or other such systems of thought, these philosophies differ from the basic materialistic view which I have just been describing in that they positively attack the Christian gospel and its concept of God. Anything that smacks of the supernatural they have vowed to destroy. Whereas materialism ignores God, atheism attacks God. In one sense the exponents of atheism are more easy to deal with, because they have the intelligence to see that man is essentially a religious being. They recognize that man must have his religion. Whether you call it communism or humanism or, to quote Sir Julian Huxley, 'religion without revelation,' even the atheist must have a religion. These atheistic philosophers are deliberately trying to replace the old supernatural religion with a new religion, and they know it and admit it. In their new religion there is a new deity, the deity of human reason. There are new processes, new methods of worship and new means of promulgating the atheistic gospel.

We can therefore meet these people on their own ground because it is a question of one ideology against another. As I said before, this makes atheism considerably easier to deal with than the sheer dead weight of materialism.

3. Attacks from within Christendom

The third direction from which attack comes is from within Christendom. We are all familiar with the way in which Satan's attack on the early church was first from without, then from within and then once more from without, and so on. In this biblical tradition, unhappily, we have to defend the Scriptures from attacks originating within Christendom. I do not need to elaborate upon this because it is not my subject here. The fact that much of Christendom has abandoned a belief in the inspiration and authority of Scripture is self-evident and known to us well. Once you have rejected the doctrine of the inspiration of Scripture, then the creation stories and their contradiction of the evolutionary outlook become irrelevant. All you have to do is to choose those parts of the Bible which you can accept and reject the rest. Thus the

Bible has been totally set aside by the majority of our professing Christian churches as a source of reliable authority in matters of faith, practice and revelation, let alone as the place to seek a true account of origins.

Attacks from evangelicals
I want to spend more time on the fourth direction from which the attack comes, which is one that gives me much greater cause for concern. That is the attack upon the doctrines of Scripture that comes, unwittingly, from within the conservative evangelical camp. I want to spend time on this because I might be 'treading on toes' here and I feel I have to justify what I am about to say.

Attacks upon the Bible from within the conservative evangelical camp? Is that conceivable? Well, unfortunately I believe it is, especially in this area with which we are now concerned. I want to review this matter briefly by looking at a number of publications, some of them now quite old, which I believe are key to the matter. Some of these books, I believe, have been formative. That is to say, they have directly influenced evangelical thinking in the matter. Others are not important in that respect but simply reflect the current mood.

One which I believe to have been formative is a book by Bernard Ramm entitled *The Christian View of Science and Scripture*. Published in 1955, it was a scholarly book and therefore carried great weight. I want to quote one or two of the commendations of this book from the dust jacket, because I think we shall then see how dangerous such a book can be. This danger arises because the book, along with its erroneous teaching, contained much which was good and wholesome and true and because it was written as a sincere attempt to reconcile the conflicts between science and religion and bury them for ever.

Dr Wilbur Smith apparently wrote of this book: 'The most important discussion of the problems involved in the vast and difficult subject of modern science and the ancient scripture that has appeared in this country for the last fifty years. It is the truly epochal work, *The Christian View of Science and Scripture* by my friend Bernard Ramm. It is the only book that I know of by an evangelical scholar today that can favourably be compared with the masterly learned works in this field which were produced in the latter part of the nineteenth century. This truly remarkable volume is the best that our evangelical world has yet produced in our day.'

Dr Harold Ockenga of Boston said, 'Sane, objective, constructive, scholarly and biblical, it fearlessly faces the provincialism of fundamentalism whilst sternly adhering to the great fundamentals of the Faith.'

Dr Billy Graham wrote, 'While I have accepted the verbal inspiration of Scripture by faith, Dr Ramm's book strengthens my intellectual acceptance. He gives logical and conclusive reasons for the hope that is within us. While I cannot say that I can agree with every point, I must commend it as the outstanding book that has come into my hands in the last few months.'

I could provide you with further quotations, but I think these are sufficient to show that this book was widely accepted by the Christian public and by Christian leaders at the time of its publication. Indeed, it was hailed as a profound expression of evangelical belief, yet when we come to examine what the book teaches we find serious departures from conservative theology. Here are one or two extracts. Naturally I am picking the particular passages which illustrate my point, but they are none the less telling for that.

'Hyper-orthodoxy' (which I suspect describes my own position!) 'does not believe its platform to the hilt. It is willing to retain faith in the Bible no matter what the scientists say. But would they really believe the Bible if at every point the Bible and science conflicted?' The implication here is, plainly, that we are only allowed to believe the Bible as long as it is in agreement with science. If we carry on believing the Bible when it appears to conflict with scientific theories we are called 'hyper-orthodox'.

Here is just a single but typical sentence: 'We also have reliable knowledge of millions of years of geological history; exhaustive researches have been made.' So he accepts, without any question or discussion, the geological time-scale that is presented to us by uniformitarian geology.

Ramm quotes, with favour, C. W. Shields: 'Take the Bible without astronomy and there would remain the infinite and absolute Jehovah enthroned in the skies of our little planet as the only scene of his abode.' I refute that totally. I do not agree for one moment that this is the picture the Bible gives of God. Even Solomon declared, 'Heaven and the highest heaven cannot contain thee.' I do not see there the parochial view of God that Shields ascribes to the Bible. The quotation continues: 'But bring the two together (i.e. Scripture and astronomy) and at once the Author of Scripture becomes the Author of Nature with all his revealed attributes in full manifestation . . . Astronomy thus yields overwhelming evidence in favour of real religion.' Now, I understand the sincerity of the writer in penning these words. I understand what he is driving at and I sympathize with it to some extent. But he is treading on extremely thin ice because the implication is that revelation needs to be bolstered up, supported and evidenced by science. That is the slippery slope down which I believe these writers have begun to slide and from which it is very difficult to escape.

Here is another quotation from the same book: 'The book of nature and the Word of God emanate from the same infallible Author and therefore cannot be at variance; but man is a fallible interpreter and by mistaking one or both of these Divine Records he forces them often into unnatural conflict.' You notice that the book of nature and the Word of God are both 'Divine Records'. They are put on a par, on an equal level, so that one is not to be preferred or advanced beyond the other. This surely is a denial of the evangelical doctrine of Scripture and the teaching of Romans 1 concerning the inability of fallen man to comprehend the 'book of nature'.

The attitude to the miraculous in this book is frankly that of escapism, an attempt to explain away that which is miraculous, although the author constantly pleads a totally different attitude. The geological record, as presently interpreted, is preferred to the historicity of the book of Genesis. Ramm rejects a literal interpretation of Genesis 1 and he also rejects any possibility of the universality of the flood: 'The universality of the flood,' he concludes after a long argument, 'simply means the universality of the experience of the man who reported it.' This is a plain contradiction of numerous Scriptures, for example, Genesis 6:7, 13, 17; 7:4, 21-23; 8:21; 2 Peter 3:6. We shall look further at this point in the following chapter.

Well, there is a book commended by Christian leaders in glowing terms, which has, I believe, profoundly influenced evangelical Christian thought.

In 1959 another book was published. It marked the centenary of Darwin's *Origin of Species* and it is entitled *Evolution and Christian Thought Today*, edited by Dr Russell Mixter of Wheaton College. Again we find the same tendencies. The historicity of Genesis is rejected in such terms as these: 'Before we examine this material it is of the utmost importance that the nature of biblical language be understood. Biblical language is not the precise language of modern-day science. It is popular, phenomenal and oftentimes poetical. Thus we are not to look for intricate detail but for basic underlying principles. It is also well to be reminded that the Bible's main aim is to tell us who made the universe and not how it was made.' I wonder how the writer can substantiate a claim of that sort in the light of the relevant Scriptures. He continues: 'These remarks apply particularly to the early chapters of Genesis for recent researches into ancient literature assure us that these passages are not to be interpreted literally but poetically or allegorically.'

On the origin of life we find that the authors (and this is a volume edited by the Professor of Zoology at Wheaton College, Illinois) give complete credence to the concepts of chemical evolution which, as a scientist, I have no hesitation in rejecting totally: 'It does mean that reputable scientists do have faith that life arose from inanimate matter through a series of physico-chemical processes no different from those we can observe today. If Christians cannot accept this at least as a legitimate hypothesis there will inevitably be conflict at this point.' Well, the writer speaks truly enough there!

Under the heading 'A Christian view of the origin of life' we read as follows: 'Many devout Christians have found little difficulty in accepting the evidence for the age of the earth presented in an earlier chapter, and the gradual development of living forms to be discussed in subsequent chapters, regarding this as an illustration of God's use of natural forces in a process of continuous creative activity.' To me that sounds exactly like the materialistic world-view I have first described. It is certainly not a 'Christian view of the origin of life'.

I want now to come to another book. In 1965, the Inter-Varsity Fellowship published a book of essays entitled *Christianity in a Mechanistic Universe*, edited by Professor MacKay. In this book, there is advanced what is called 'the principle of complementarity'. This was not an original idea, but I believe the book brought it forward and made the Christian public aware of it in a new way and with new force.

Very simply, complementarity suggests that there are two distinct and self-consistent descriptions, or explanations, of the universe and of nature: the theological and the scientific. On one side we have a scientific description of the universe which is totally self-consistent and complete and in which the concept of God is irrelevant and unnecessary. On the other side, we have the theological interpretation and explanation of life which we find in the Bible. Both are true and the whole truth can only be obtained by holding the two as separate but complementary views of the universe. So runs the argument.

Once again those involved in advancing these views are sincerely attempting to solve some of the problems and resolve some of the conflicts between Christianity and science. Why should we disagree with them? What is wrong with complementarity?

The first fault that I find with this view is that it encourages the construction of a world-view without God, as an alternative to the biblical world-view. It deliberately encourages the formulation of the materialistic philosophy that I referred to earlier. It says, 'Yes by all means construct an account of creation and of life and of being that ignores God, but remember that when you have done this, it is only one of two complementary views.' The illustration is given of a painting. You can describe that painting either in terms of the artist's intentions and the message that he is seeking to convey, in terms of the subjective influence and impact it has upon the viewer, or you can describe it in scientific terms. You can analyse each point of the picture and specify its chemical composition and thereby give a total and complete and perfect description of the picture in terms of scientific formulae without any reference to the purpose of the artist or its subjective or aesthetic effect upon the viewer. This is a very persuasive illustration, but we must not, we dare not, encourage the construction of a godless world-view. For having developed that world-view it will be accepted by those around us, and when we say, 'Just a minute, you have to have the other view as well,' their reaction will be 'No thank you very much; we are quite happy with this.'

The second fault I find with complementarity is that it suggests that science *is* a self-contained system, and I would deny that that is true. I am a scientist and I earn my living and my reputation by the practice of science, but I would state in the strongest possible terms that science is not self-contained. Science offers only half an explanation of nature, because while it is possible to explain all kinds of phenomena and observations in terms of scientific law, it is quite *impossible* to explain *scientific law* itself! That is what I mean when I say that science is only half an explanation. To suggest that in some way a scientific description of the universe is complete and can stand in its own right as a self-contained system of thought is, in my opinion, quite false.

Thirdly, the principle of complementarity leaves the doctrines of creation, providence and the miraculous in a kind of limbo, because it has divorced and separated the spiritual from the material. Perhaps we could recognize in this divorce a latter-day gnosticism, but that might be unkind. But it certainly leaves us with nowhere to put the doctrines of providence and creation, as is evident from the quotations I have given you. The complementarians are really at a loss to know what to do with the doctrine of creation and they dare not mention miracles, because these doctrines involve interaction between the two 'spheres' which complementarity so assiduously separates.

The faults, then, of our evangelical brethren who subscribe to these views may be summed up as follows. They have, first of all, a tendency to see science and revelation as parallel, equivalent or alternative views of the universe instead of ceding superiority to revelation. Secondly, their view discounts entirely the biblical testimony on the shortcomings of human wisdom. It seems to me that they have not read 1 Corinthians 1 and 2. They give an almost unbelievable degree of credence to anything that is said or stated or claimed in the name of science. They yield the ground before it is even disputed. They forget that science itself is an interpretation of observations and that those interpretations are subject to the fallibility of fallen human nature. The facts of observation generally are not disputed. The interpretations we put upon those facts are, and indeed should be, hotly disputed whenever those interpretations contradict the doctrines of the Word of God. Finally, they fail to understand the nature of science and the nature of the miraculous. We shall return to that in just a moment.

The answer

I want to be positive at this point since up till now I have been, to some extent, destructive. You will remember that Nehemiah had to clear away the rubbish before he could start building the walls of Jerusalem; similarly there is always a destructive work to be done on false or mistaken ideas before we can start rebuilding with

sound ones. But, as I said at the beginning, it is not sufficient for us
to be destructive. It is not sufficient just to snipe at our opponents in this matter. We have to answer in a positive way. We
have to present, positively and strongly, the biblical viewpoint as
a complete theory of being that will satisfy the keenest intellects,
will give a proper place to scientific investigation, will recognize in
science a great source of benefit to mankind, but will not elevate
science or any other form of human intellectual endeavour to the
same level as revelation.

So then, what is our answer? I believe first of all that we (and I
am addressing fellow Christian workers, ministers of the gospel,
and indeed all Christians) must return again to a clear and un-
equivocal proclamation of the superiority of revelation to reason. I
feel that we have too often been ashamed to challenge from the
Scripture the views that I have just been criticizing. We have tried
to avoid them. We have welcomed ideas such as complementarity
because they seemed to separate the contestants and eliminate the
conflict, and in spite of the unbiblical character of these ideas we
have been content and comfortable with this situation. But we
have to return to the attack. We have to return to a clear and un-
equivocal declaration that revelation is superior to reason.

We have to take up those considerable passages of Scripture
that, starting with the doctrine of the Fall of man, point to the un-
reliability of human reason and therefore of any materialistic system or world-view based upon human reason. 'Where is the wise
man? Where is the scribe? Where is the debater of this age? Has
not God made foolish the wisdom of the world?'

Now in doing this we must avoid the charge of being obscuran-
tists. As we saw in chapter 1, we are not dismissing human reason
and wisdom. Remember how Paul goes on in 1 Corinthians 2 to
say, 'Yet we do speak wisdom.' Paul is very quick to indicate that
he is not setting reason and rationality aside. 'Yet we do speak
wisdom,' but it is not the wisdom of this world. It is a wisdom in
which human rationality and intellect work upon the data of revelation to lead us to a deeper knowledge of God. It is quite evident
from a cursory reading of the New Testament that we are not trying to set reason aside, or oppose reason, or say that faith is irrational. God forbid! It is quite evident that the use of rational argument in Scripture is itself a denial of that accusation. What we
are saying is that reason must bow to revelation. We are saying
that you can only have one ultimate authority. Either that author-

ity is revelation, and human reason must bow to revelation where it cannot reconcile that revelation with its own limited, fallen insights, or else we must make human reason the final court of appeal, and where human reason cannot comprehend or reconcile the statements of Scripture then Scripture must give way. You cannot have it both ways, yet I feel that some of our brethren whose views I have been quoting are guilty of trying to do so. They are trying to have an inspired and authoritative revelation, but they are only prepared to have it as long as they can understand it in every detail, in every particular and reconcile every observation and interpretation of science with that revelation.

We must recognize that science itself is a series of interpretations, as I have argued more fully in chapter 2. We must not accept as the final word what scientists say, what they theorize and what they *deduce* from the facts of observation. So often scientists have to go back and retract what they have said and reinterpret the facts. We do not dispute the facts, but we very often and very properly dispute the interpretations that are sometimes placed upon those facts. In a sense the scientist is open to exactly the same accusation that is hurled at the 'hyper-orthodox'. That is to say, his facts may be correct but his interpretations wrong. The Bible is true but our interpretations are wrong, they say. We interpret it literally when it should be interpreted poetically or allegorically. Well, exactly the same kind of accusation can be laid at the door of science. Scientific theories are interpretations of the facts, not the facts themselves. Wherever those interpretations are made in the absence of a regenerate and enlightened mind, they will inevitably fall short of the whole truth.

Secondly, we must proclaim the biblical doctrine of nature in greater depth. I am going to coin a phrase (I think I am coining it rather than borrowing it) namely, 'the theology of science'. Do we have a theology of science? And if we do not, why not? After all, every aspect of human experience is subject to its own branch of theology. We have, for example, a theology (that is simply to say a God-centred view or interpretation) of history, do we not? We proclaim that history is the unfolding of God's purposes. And yet there is no greater factor in human life and education today than science. It is one of the foremost thought-modes, bodies of knowledge and areas of human endeavour of our time. I feel, therefore, that we have failed as evangelicals by not going to our Bibles to work out a theology of science. We tend to think that since it is not religion or theology, we are not concerned with it in the teaching of Christian doctrine. We consider science to be simply irrelevant. I sympathize, of course, with those ministers and preachers who have had no scientific training, but let us face the fact that the majority of young people today get a reasonably adequate exposure to the basic concepts and approaches of science and, unfortunately, to the wholly false idea that science and biblical faith are incompatible. We need, therefore, a theology of science.

I believe that a very simple and clear theology of science can be deduced from the Scriptures. I would point you to such verses as Colossians 1:17 and Hebrews 1:2, 3, where we are told that Christ, the second person of the Trinity, 'upholds all things by the word of his power' and that 'by him all things hold together'. With those two verses alone, together perhaps with Acts 17:25–28 and the great teachings of the doctrine of providence in the Old Testament, we can construct a theology of science. We can point out that the scientific laws to which all science is ultimately reduced *are* the word of God's power. That is, I believe, what the Bible means by the statement that he upholds all things by the word of his power. This verse refers to the rules or laws which operate in nature and by which this 'scientific' world is seen to work. The laws of science are the commands of God operating moment by moment. In him we live and move and exist and so also does all life and all material existence. By this biblical reasoning we provide an underpinning for science, a reason for science, a basis for science, an explanation of science. And immediately, far from separating science from religion, and a scientific world-view from a theological world-view (as the doctrine of complementarity seeks to do) we bring them together, we unite them, we synthesize them into a single grand and glorious picture of a sovereign God who, in total immediacy, is Ruler of heaven and earth. We must understand that science is derivative from God. If we do that we shall provide ourselves with a positive framework in which we can reinterpret science in a biblical and God-centred manner.

The third part of my answer follows from the second. We must reinstate the rationality of the miraculous in our preaching and teaching. One of the most tragic things about these books that I have been quoting is that although they pretend to accept the Scriptures as being inspired, they bend over backwards to explain away every miracle that they possibly can, in terms of naturalistic and scientific occurrences. We must not be ashamed of the miraculous; we have to realize that the whole gospel is based upon the miraculous. 'If Christ has not been raised,' says Paul, 'then our preaching is in vain, your faith also is in vain . . . you are still in your sins.' We must stop being apologetic about the miraculous element in Scripture.

It seems to me that most of this discussion arises because Christians who pretend to accept the Bible as infallible are ashamed of the miraculous element in it and so, of course, they just dispute the historicity of Genesis. Only by saying that creation was miraculous can you substantiate and support the historicity of Genesis, and we are afraid to do it. We are frightened of being considered superstitious. But let us realize that the supernatural and the miraculous lie at the very heart of our gospel and we must not be ashamed to proclaim them.

I said that we must reinstate the rationality of the miraculous. What exactly do I mean by this? I think that much of our embarrassment over the miraculous comes from a failure to understand our Bibles on the subject. So often evangelicals have interpreted the miraculous in terms of God's *intervention* in the natural order. We have painted a picture of a universe that runs and operates according to scientific law, with God remote and external to that universe. In this false view, God has left the universe running smoothly according to scientific principles and only interferes from time to time to produce miraculous events. Well, of course, this makes God nothing more than a meddler.

The theology of science to which I have just referred leads us to a completely different view of miracles, namely the concept that God is present now, upholding all things by the word of his power; that every operation of scientific law is the present-tense purpose and design of God. This concept opens the way for a rational understanding of the miraculous. As long as we think of God as someone standing outside the material universe, occasionally coming in just to interfere, we shall not have a very persuasive doctrine of the miraculous. If, however, we recognize that the *normal* processes of scientific law are a manifestation of the presence and activity of God ('for in him we live and move and exist'), we find that the miraculous is no longer an act of intervention at all. We find rather that the miraculous is qualitatively exactly the same thing as the non-miraculous!

Let me explain what I mean by giving you an illustration. Every morning of every working day I travel from my home in

Hertfordshire to my office in London University. If some observer watched my travelling habits, he would very quickly be able to deduce the 'laws' or rules which control my travelling. He would observe that Monday to Friday at a certain time each morning I leave my home and make my way to the railway station. I catch a certain train and I follow a certain route to my office. He might observe that this does not happen two mornings a week, and so on. Thus by gathering data he would construct a law which describes my behaviour. This is analogous to the way a scientist might construct a law describing the behaviour of atoms or molecules or electrical discharges or any other scientific phenomenon. But occasionally, when there is good reason for it, I travel by car. Very rarely do I do this, but there may be some special reason for needing a car in London and so I travel by car. This breaks my habit of travelling by train. It is an exception to the rule that the observer has so carefully constructed and written down. That is like a miracle happening which contravenes, or sets aside for a moment, localized in time and space, the normal operation of scientific law.

The point I want to bring home is this: that even though I usually travel by train there is each morning the positive decision, conscious or unconscious, to use one or other mode of transport. Just because ninety-nine times out of a hundred I travel by train, it does not mean that my journey does not represent a conscious decision each morning to do so. So, qualitatively, travelling by train or travelling by car are really quite identical. They both represent the outcome of conscious decision on my part. It is only quantitatively that one seems so different from the other, because I nearly always travel by train and only rarely by car.

Like all illustrations, no doubt this one has serious inadequacies, but I think it helps us to understand the nature of the miraculous. When normal scientific law operates it does so by the conscious, moment by moment, purpose and decision of God, because God is continually upholding all things by the word of his power. When a miracle occurs, it represents just the same kind of conscious decision by God as that which is normal, namely, a decision that what is normal should be set aside for that which is extraordinary.

We must stop being ashamed of miracles, for the miraculous is an integral and necessary part of the gospel of Christ.

Conclusion

In this brief review, I have suggested that the attack upon the Bible comes not only from without, from an unbelieving and materialistic world, but also from within. Evangelical Christians, faced with the undoubted problems and challenges of scientific theory, have given the wrong answers. Attempting to defend the inspiration and inerrancy of Scripture they have, instead, been driven into untenable compromises which, at best, smother the Bible's true teaching on creation, providence and miracles, or, at worst, blandly contradict it. Perhaps the main reason for this unhappy state of affairs is that theologians and scientists alike have been afraid to criticize 'the sacred cow' of science.

It is our responsibility to change this state of affairs. Science is not infallible. It is not even always clever. Like all fields of human endeavour it contains within its broad boundaries both the excellent and the second-rate, and we must learn to distinguish between them.

Specifically I have suggested three ways in which we should approach the task of reconstructing the philosophical framework of our Christian view of nature. We must reassert the superiority of revelation over reason. We must work out and teach a biblical theology of science. And we must reinstate the miraculous and providential works of God as both essential to our gospel and acceptable to the rational mind. May God grant us the wisdom and energy to set about these tasks.

5.
A critique of theistic evolution

As we have just seen, many evangelical Christians, especially those with some intellectual pretensions, would claim that it is possible to uphold both the doctrine of the Bible as the inspired Word of God and at the same time to accept evolutionary theory as scientifically sound. There can, they say, be no true conflict between the two, since both are the work of God. This attempt to reconcile the theory of evolution with the teaching of the Bible is known as theistic evolution and it is this claim which we now examine. The re-interpretation of Scripture that is necessary to effect its reconciliation with evolution leads to drastic changes in our understanding of the Bible, of man and of God himself.

Two views on origins

It seems to me that one of the most important issues of today for Christians, as they seek to understand the world around them, is this question of theistic evolution. Is theistic evolution an acceptable belief, by which the Bible can be reconciled with the claims of evolutionary theory, or is the Bible-believer compelled to reject these claims in favour of an ascientific theory of 'creationism'?

The reason why this is a very important matter is that large numbers of Bible-believing Christians do subscribe (wrongly, I believe) to the theory of theistic evolution and this affects their entire outlook. The distinction between these two alternative views of origins is therefore one which every Christian needs to consider.

Those who do not accept the biblical record, who are atheists or agnostic regarding the Christian faith, do not, of course, have the problems we are going to discuss in this chapter. They dismiss the testimony of Scripture regarding these matters and are happy to follow their own man-made theories concerning origins. But those of us who believe the Bible must take its teachings into consideration. Whatever our particular understanding of the means of creation, we are bound to listen to what the Bible has to say upon the subject of origins. This has the effect of dividing Christians into two camps, namely those who subscribe to theistic evolution and those who embrace creationism.

We ought therefore to begin by outlining the general nature of these two viewpoints. Creationism claims that creation was accomplished miraculously, that is, by means that have no natural or scientific explanation. 'No,' replies theistic evolution. 'Creation was not miraculous. God employed natural process, namely the process of evolution, to bring about the created order.' It is clear, of course, that theistic evolution does not exclude miracle totally from the creation process. It has to accept (as indeed even atheism has to accept) that the beginning of all things, the initial creation of matter, energy, space, time and natural law, was a 'miraculous' event. That is, it was an event that by its very nature can never be described as a consequence of natural process. Of course, the atheist says that this origin of all things was simply a unique event inaccessible to science, an inexplicable singularity for which there is no need to invoke the idea of God. On the other hand, the theistic evolutionist recognizes God as the ultimate cause of all. Indeed all Christians will agree that the origin of the universe is correctly described as a miraculous event in which God brought the elements of the universe into being *ex nihilo*, that is, out of nothing.

We might note here that attempts are being made currently to provide a scientific description of the *ex nihilo* origin itself. According to these theories, pairs of fundamental particles came into being spontaneously, one of each pair being composed of matter and one of anti-matter. This is not all that different from the now discarded theory of continuous creation propounded by Hoyle and others some thirty years ago. However, all such theories leave unresolved the creation of space and time and of natural law. Even if true, therefore, they would not represent in any way an explanation of the beginning of the universe.

Having agreed that the original creation was miraculous, at least in the sense that it is incapable of scientific explanation, theistic evolution proceeds to state that all subsequent events, including the remainder of the creation, were accomplished by natural process, that is, by some form of evolution controlled only by the laws of nature that operate today. In contrast, creationism maintains that creation is described in Scripture as a succession of creative fiats, embracing, among other things, the formation of the earth, the origin of life and the creation of man.

So, then, we have a choice, and the main purpose of this chapter is to demonstrate that the choice we make affects not only our view of creation, but the whole of our Christian outlook. It affects things which are far more immediate and important to us than the past events which gave rise to the natural world. In particular we shall examine the way it influences our interpretation of Scripture, our understanding of man and our view of God.

The interpretation of Scripture

We shall look in turn at creationism and theistic evolution and see how they affect the way we interpret Scripture. Considering creationism first, let us begin by clearing up a number of possible misunderstandings of the creationist position.

First of all, creationism does not insist on a completely literal in-terpretation of the Bible. It calls rather for a *literary* interpretation. Let me explain. The word 'literal' creates all kinds of difficulties in people's minds. Usually, those who oppose the creationist view-point attach the label 'literalist' to the creationist and then use this assignation to ridicule him. But this is wholly unfair, for the creationist makes no such claim. Indeed, if we try to interpret the Bible literally at all points we find ourselves in all kinds of trouble, for a literal statement is a statement of precise fact, or as close to that as human language will allow.

Consider, by way of example, the repeated statement in Genesis 1 of the words, 'God said'. We read, 'God said, "Let there be light" ', 'God said, ". . . Let the dry land appear" ', and so on. The result of God's 'saying' was, of course, that certain stages in the creation were accomplished. Now, a literal interpretation would require us to believe that these words were pronounced by God in an audible voice and in some known or unknown lan-guage. An imaginary observer would have heard the actual sound of spoken words. We all recognize, however, that the idea of God speaking has a far more general connotation. We read that God spoke to man in his Son (Heb. 1:2). Psalm 33 tells us that 'By the word of the Lord the heavens were made, and by the breath of his mouth all their host,' and again, 'He spoke, and it was done; he commanded, and it stood fast' (Ps. 33:6,9). Psalm 50:1 proclaims, 'The Mighty One, God, the Lord, has spoken, and summoned the earth from the rising of the sun to its setting.'

We have to recognize that the Bible frequently employs anthropomorphism, that is, it pictures God acting as a human being. In speaking, therefore, God is pictured as a ruler, uttering sovereign commands which are then carried out unquestioningly by his minions; as a military commander issuing orders to his armies. This is straightforward anthropomorphism and in such instances no literal speech is implied, but rather an exercise of divine will and power. God's speaking in Scripture therefore signifies his control and command over things and events. It is a metaphor denoting the power and control that God exercises over the created order. It is not a literality, requiring an audible voice, although, of course, God could have used such a voice had he chosen! The point to grasp is that the word 'spoke' implies something far more significant in its metaphorical form than in its literal meaning, and this is clearly the import of God's speaking in Genesis 1.

This rather trivial case of non-literality was chosen deliberately to show how often human language employs metaphor and other literary means without our really noticing it. Much of the richness of language derives from this very fact. But let us now consider another, more important, case where we must adopt a non-literal interpretation, namely in explaining the contrast between the first and second chapters of Genesis. In the first chapter we are told plainly that animals were created before man. The sequence is quite explicit. If we turn to the second chapter, however, we find that man was apparently created before animals, for that is the order in which their respective creations are presented. If we interpret these chapters in a wholly literal manner, we have a difficult contradiction on our hands and one which the opponents of biblical truth are quick to point out.

Once again, however, we recognize that a literary, rather than a literal, interpretation is in order. That is, a dramatic device is being employed in Genesis 2 and one with which we are familiar in modern literature. The device in question is 'flash-back', in which the order of events is deliberately reversed to provide dramatic impact or interest. This is clearly what has happened in Genesis 2. This chapter is an account of creation in which man is central. Genesis 1 presents the creation as a whole and man arrives on the scene only at the culmination of the creative process. Genesis 2, on the other hand, is all about man. It tells the story of creation from a man-centred viewpoint. Because man is the dominant theme in Genesis 2, it is his creation which is first mentioned. Having introduced the principal character, the author goes on to relate man to the remainder of creation, dealing in turn with the garden (man's primeval environment), the animal kingdom (man's fellow creatures) and, finally, the relationship between man and woman. The sequence is intended to be logical rather than chronological, as the writer works out the theme of human relationships and their origin.

We see, therefore, that there are different literary forms employed in Genesis 1 and 2. We recognize that the Bible uses literary devices such as metaphor, simile, anthropomorphism and dramatic forms to convey its message. The reason for this rich variety of language is basically that we must always describe the unknown in terms of the known. Otherwise we could never learn any truth concerning the invisible things of God. What is true of these first two chapters of Genesis is also true on the larger scale, and we find that whole passages and even books of the Bible present truth in poetical, allegorical and even apocalyptical dress.

Having established, then, that we do not necessarily interpret Scripture in a slavishly literal manner, but rather according to its literary genre and therefore according to the intention of the author, we nevertheless insist that those passages where the form and content are historical must be interpreted as genuine history. To do so is only to be consistent. For if a literary interpretation (rather than a literal one) correctly conveys the intention of the writer, we must also follow his intention as regards the character of the passage, whether it is fact or fiction.

When we turn to such passages as Genesis 1 to 3, and to the flood narrative, for example, we find that their contents are presented plainly as historical fact. Those facts may be expressed using a variety of dramatic and literary devices, but the author nevertheless claims to be relating events that actually took place. The narratives are accounts, not of myth, but of reality. So then, creationism adopts a historical approach to these historical portions of Scripture.

In contrast, the theistic evolutionist is forced by his view of origins to interpret Scripture in a rather different manner. His need to reconcile the Bible with an evolutionary scenario, without rejecting the authority of either, constrains him to follow a somewhat tortuous path. How does he go about it? Let us exemplify this by reference, first of all, to Genesis 1.

We have already seen that the opening verse, 'In the beginning God created the heavens and the earth,' is taken by the theistic evolutionist to be a factual and historical statement. He accepts this verse as history. However, he then becomes totally inconsistent by saying that everything which follows this opening verse is non-historical, void of historical significance or relevance. This *volte-face* is unavoidable because there is so much in Genesis 1 that contradicts evolutionary theory if taken in a straightforward historical sense. So much so, in fact, that it is difficult for the theistic evolutionist to concede that there is any historically reliable information in Genesis 1 after the first verse. It must all be interpreted as mythology, that is, as a non-historical vehicle for spiritual truth. On this view, then, we are not to understand 'days' as being actual days; the events recorded there did not actually take place; the sequence described is not the actual sequence in which the various biological forms appeared on earth, and so on. The whole account provides nothing more than a bland declaration that God created the heavens and the earth by some means and in some manner that is not even hinted at in the chapter. There is no factual information to be found whatever in this, the foundational chapter of the Bible.

A second example of the way theistic evolution handles Scripture concerns the opening verses of Genesis 2. This involves a rejection of the plain meaning (indeed, of any meaning!) of the text. In these verses we are told quite specifically, and with some emphasis, that God finished his work of creation and rested on the seventh day. He ceased from 'all his work which God had created and made'. Now that, it seems to me, is as plain a statement as one could wish for that creation was completed, that an era came to an end, that a mode in which God had been dealing with the cosmos was terminated and superseded by another, different mode. So significant was this event in biblical terms that the seven-day week and the Jewish sabbath were instituted to commemorate it.

Not so, says theistic evolution. It believes instead that there was no change, for creation was brought about by natural process which continues unaltered today. The events of creation 'week' were in no way different to those that have occurred ever since.

Evolution brought animals and man alike into being (events included biblically in creation week) but evolution has continued unabated since, continuing to produce new life forms right up to the present day. Since we are discussing *theistic* evolution, of course, it is admitted that natural process is directed by God. But God's sovereignty over natural process is providence and providence is operative today. It has not ceased and cannot therefore be the subject of Genesis 2:1-3.

If it be maintained that the creation described in Genesis 1 occurred by providential means rather than by miraculous fiat, if only providence was at work before the seventh day and only providence was at work after it, then nothing ceased on the seventh day and Genesis 2:1-3 is, at best, meaningless and, at worst, a lie. As it happens, I have never seen a theistic evolutionary explanation of these verses, nor can I see how any could be advanced. The plain meaning of Genesis 2 is that on the seventh day God completed a series of creative acts and thereafter deals with the universe in a fundamentally different manner, that is, through natural process guided by providence (though the Bible testifies to periodic episodes of the miraculous throughout human history). Evolution, by contrast, is an ongoing process which continues unabated from the dawn of the cosmos to this day. It can allow no essential change of mode, no cessation of the creative process, no seventh day. Metaphorically speaking, therefore, the theistic evolutionist has to cut Genesis 2:1-3 out of his Bible since for him nothing has ceased, nothing has changed; there is nothing from which God rested . . . if evolution is true.

A final illustration of the way theistic evolution distorts the interpretation of Scripture concerns the flood of Noah's day. Because evolution ascribes the fossil record to natural processes occurring over long periods of time (processes of sedimentation, erosion, consolidation, uplift, overthrust, etc., needing hundreds of millennia to accomplish), it leaves no place in the geological record for evidence of a cataclysmic, world-wide flood such as the Bible describes in Genesis 6-9. Since there is no record of such a flood (once one has attributed the entire geological column to some other cause), the event has to be downgraded. According to theistic evolution, therefore, there could not have been a worldwide inundation. All life on earth could not possibly have perished during a short period. Therefore the Genesis flood must have been some geologically insignificant local event which the writer has magnified out of all proportion to the original reality.

If we turn to Genesis 7, however, we can pick out many statements which flatly contradict this scenario. 'The water prevailed more and more upon the earth . . . all the high mountains everywhere under the heavens were covered. The water prevailed fifteen cubits higher, and the mountains were covered. And all flesh that moved on the earth perished... Thus he blotted out every living thing [literally 'all existence'] that was upon the face of the land . . . only Noah was left, together with those that were with him in the ark' (Gen. 7: 19-23).

Theistic evolutionists argue that the repeated use of the word 'all' does not necessarily indicate universality. Perhaps it was only that region of the world then inhabited by man that was destroyed? Does not the New Testament use similar terminology in Luke 2:1 where Caesar decreed that a census be taken of 'all the inhabited earth'? Hardly. The Greek word used here is much clearer than the Authorized Version's 'all the world'. It is based on the word for 'house' or dwelling and plainly signifies a region of known habitation. The decree was for a general taxation rather than a local one and the context makes the meaning clear. There is no comparison, therefore, with the language used in Genesis to describe the universality of the flood: 'The end of all flesh is come before me . . . behold, I am about to destroy them with the earth . . . everything that is on the earth shall perish' (Gen. 6:13, 17). Both the Hebrew word for 'ground' and that for 'earth' are employed in these global pronouncements, the latter being the word used in Genesis 1:1 of the created earth.

But quite apart from the words used, the whole emphasis of the Genesis account of the flood precludes the idea of a merely local event. The need for the animals to be protected in the ark points to universality, for the effects of a local flood could soon be eliminated by recolonization. God's covenant with Noah recorded in Genesis 9:9-17 was also a covenant with 'every living creature of all flesh that is on the earth'. God promised that water should never 'again . . . become a flood to destroy all flesh'. Moreover, what are we to make of the promise that 'seedtime and harvest . . . shall not cease' (Gen. 8:22) if the context were not that of a universal flood? For seedtime and harvest have frequently failed on a *local* scale! It is only on a global scale that this promise was made and remains true to this day. Finally, we are told that from the three sons of Noah 'the whole earth was populated' (Gen.

9:19). Certainly the Bible teaches that all mankind apart from
Noah and his family were killed (see also 1 Peter 3:20; 2 Peter
3:6).

In spite of the clear testimony of Scripture, theistic evolutionists
are compelled by their belief to reject the plain meaning of the
texts and impose upon them a principle of interpretation that is
external to the Bible, namely that it must be reconciled with
evolution. They argue that *all* interpretation, in the final analysis,
involves reading the Bible in the light of our personal understanding and experience and that evolutionary theory is part of that experience for the modern man. But evolutionary theory is just what
it says, a theory of origins. It is *not* part of real life experience in the
way that the exact sciences are (since their theories can be tested
in the laboratory).

The historical evangelical position is that it is never correct to
impose upon the Bible an external principle of interpretation,
however ingenious or intellectually satisfying it might be. Such interpretations are the inventions of man and not the revelation of
God. The only correct way to approach Scripture is to use internal
criteria or principles of interpretation, to interpret one part of
Scripture by another. Although theistic evolutionists often pay
lip-service to this principle, I believe that their approach is, in fact,
a denial of it. Plainly, our view of origins affects our interpretation
and use of Scripture.

What is man?

The second major subject that is affected by theistic evolution is
our understanding of man. The creationist understands the narrative of Genesis 1 and 2 to describe the unique creation of a single
man and woman. Adam and Eve were not beings whose bodies
were prepared in some way by a process of evolution; they did not
emerge from apehood, but were special creations of God. According to the creationist, man was not derived from pre-existing animal stock, but directly from 'dust from the ground', a physical
being indeed, but one made also in the image of God. By 'image',
of course, we do not mean a physical representation, for God is
Spirit. We mean, rather, that from the moment of his creation
man reflected the rational, spiritual and moral character of
his Maker. Furthermore, he shared with God the attribute of
immortality.

The man thus created was given a certain commandment by God. He was not to take the fruit of the tree that stood at the centre of the garden. Adam and Eve disobeyed that instruction and, in consequence, were thrust out of Eden. They suffered the punishment of death and brought its curse upon all their descendants, the whole human race. This death was not, of course, instantaneous. They did not drop dead beneath the tree, even though God had said, 'In the day that you take of the fruit you shall die.' How are we to understand this warning, therefore? In two ways, says the creationist. First of all they suffered spiritual death. There is testimony throughout the Bible to the effect that man is by nature spiritually dead. He is cut off from God, unable to communicate with him, dead in trespasses and sins. The essence of the gospel is that men and women who are dead in sins may be brought back to spiritual life by the power of God, by the work of the Spirit and through the merits of Jesus Christ.

Spiritual death was, therefore, a consequence of the fall of Adam, but not the only one. At that time man became subject to physical death also. It seems to me that this is made very clear in Scripture: 'In the day that you eat . . ., you shall surely die.' In the instant of his disobedience man lost his immortality, dying in the sense that he became mortal. This is the burden of Paul's words in 1 Corinthians 15:22 where we read, 'As in Adam all die, so in Christ all shall be made alive.'

The immediate context of this statement is the resurrection of *the body*. It is resurrection in the sense that Christ rose from the dead on the third day (1 Cor. 15:12,13). Much of Paul's argument makes nonsense if he is discussing anything other than physical resurrection (e.g. 1 Cor. 15:29,35). It is not therefore possible to read this as 'As in Adam all die spiritually, so in Christ shall all be made alive physically.' That would be to reverse the meaning intended by the apostle. Read the whole chapter and you will find that the meaning is unambiguous. Paul's argument is that just as all humans are subject to physical death on account of Adam's transgression, so all believers will be made alive physically at the resurrection in the last times. See also Romans 8:23 and 1 Thessalonians 4:13-18. We also know from other scriptures, such as Revelation 20:5-15, that all men, whether believers or not, will participate in physical resurrection.

It is true that the resurrection body will be a 'spiritual' rather than a 'natural' body (1 Cor. 15:44), but it is nevertheless to be a *body*. The eternal heavenly state of believers, Paul tells us in Philippians 3:20,21, will be a corporeal existence in which the earthly body has been transformed 'into conformity with the body of [Christ's] glory'. Thus the doctrine of the physical resurrection is firmly entrenched in the New Testament and inextricably linked with the resurrection of Christ and his return in glory. This only makes sense if physical death was the consequence of Adam's sin, not a merely natural event having no special significance in the eyes of God.

Let us now consider how theistic evolution deals with the nature and origin of man. First of all, evolution does not see human origins in terms of one unique individual, Adam, and his equally unique wife. According to evolution, it is not individuals that evolve, but populations. Whether we think of amoeba, mice or men, it is not the individual that climbs dramatically up the ladder of evolutionary development, but the population as a whole. No accepted evolutionary theory claims that evolution occurs at the level of the individual, though Goldschmidt's 'hopeful monster' or saltation hypothesis did adopt essentially this position. Even those who have revived his ideas, however, like the exponents of punctuated equilibrium, speak in terms of rapidly evolving populations rather than evolutionary quantum leaps in single generations.

If evolution is true, therefore, we do not have a unique individual, Adam, but rather a population of emergent humankind. Adam can only be a representative man, a kind of symbol for mankind. If this view is adopted, however, it creates great difficulties in the interpretation of certain scriptures, notably Romans 5 and 1 Corinthians 15.

We are told in Romans 5:12,15 that the consequence of Adam's sin (that is, death) 'spread to all men'. But if Adam was not the unique parent and head of the human race, the biblical argument that we inherit Adam's sinful nature falls to the ground. According to 1 Corinthians 15:22, all men die 'in Adam', that is, as a consequence of their descent from him. They all bear Adam's image, repeats 1 Corinthians 15:49. If Adam was not unique, but merely one of a population of early humans, or if he was not an individual at all, but simply a symbol of humanity, then there is no unique descent and no inheritance of fallen nature.

Pursuing this argument to its conclusion, we are forced to say that all men are not sinners because of any physical descent from a common parent, but that they have just turned out to be sinners for some unexplained reason. Adam's fall is then nothing more than a symbol of man's general tendency to disobey God. This, however, leaves us without a biblical explanation for the existence and origin of sin in man. We have turned a clear biblical account of the origin of human sin into nothing more than an assertion that all men happen to be sinners. Of course, we can still blame sin on to Satan, but the essential element of the story of the Fall (that Adam chose deliberately to disobey God and was justly punished for his rebellion) is completely lost.

Furthermore, this evolutionary scenario makes nonsense of the distinction drawn in Scripture between the respective culpabilities of Adam and Eve. We read that Eve was deceived, but that Adam, in contrast, was guilty of deliberate rebellion (1 Tim. 2:14). But if Adam's sin simply symbolizes the sin of mankind, then it also symbolizes Eve's transgression and no legitimate distinction can be made.

The second major implication of evolution is that physical death in man cannot be seen as a punishment for sin, since it was a natural feature of the animal world from which Adam evolved. The death that resulted from the fall of Adam, therefore, must be spiritual death only. We have already seen that this view is not tenable in the light of New Testament Scripture. Nor indeed is it tenable in the light of Genesis itself, for the curse pronounced upon Adam is quite explicit: 'You are dust, and to dust you shall return' (Gen. 3:19). The reference is plainly to physical death and decay and to such death as a punishment for sin.

Not only did Adam's transgression lead to his own physical mortality but also to a curse upon the entire created order. In Romans 8:20 we read that the whole creation 'was subjected to futility' by God. It became enslaved to corruption (mortality) and will only be released from this state when Christ returns to liberate his people from *their* bondage, that is, the grave.

Notice that the created order 'was subjected' to futility. It was not 'subject' to corruption as descriptive of its natural state, but was unwillingly *placed* in subjection when God 'cursed . . . the ground' for man's sake (Gen. 3:17). This demonstrates that the whole physical creation was involved in the Fall, and not just the spiritual nature of man. Man's own mortality and the deliverance that those in Christ will one day know are part of a larger reality, involving the entire physical cosmos. Any lesser view of the Fall, its consequences and its reversal at the return of Christ, cannot be biblical.

The theistic evolutionist may attempt to circumvent the problem in this way. What actually happened, he might say, is that a population of humanoid creatures began to emerge and God chose a single pair from among them. Into this pair (Adam and Eve) he put spiritual life and thus set them apart as a unique and immortal species, made 'in the image of God'. When Adam sinned, he forfeited both the spiritual life he had been given and his immortality. Although this scenario offers a compromise between special creation and evolution as they apply to man, it creates problems of its own. Firstly, of course, it rules out of court any historical reality in the account of Eve's creation from Adam's 'side' (Gen. 2:21-24). The separate origins of man and woman cannot be accommodated within any evolutionary scheme, yet the New Testament appeals to this very doctrine when dealing with the roles of men and women in the church (1 Cor. 11:7-12; 1 Tim. 2:12-15). 'It was Adam who was first created, and then Eve,' explains the apostle to Timothy.

To summarize, therefore, evolutionary scenarios for the origin of man diminish the role of Adam as the father of the human race and thus diminish the doctrines of the Fall, the resurrection of the body and the restoration of all things in Christ at his return. The concept of original sin is lost and man's sinfulness, though admitted, can no longer be traced to a historical cause. Christ's role as the 'second Adam', whose obedience undoes the evil wrought by Adam's disobedience, is also sacrificed (Rom. 5:6-21). The doctrinal cost of theistic evolution is a heavy one.

Our view of God

Finally, let us consider the views of God afforded by our two viewpoints. It is quite clear that theistic evolution claims to offer a strong doctrine of the providence of God, and its proponents often criticize creationists for being weak on this topic. Before we can assess these claims we must define what we mean by the term 'providence'.

The doctrine of providence states that God controls and overrules the natural processes of the universe to achieve his ends. He so orders and uses natural process that his purposes are fulfilled throughout the whole cosmos including, of course, human history. No doubt there are other definitions of providence which emphasize different aspects of God's sovereignty over the cosmos, but they all come down to the same thing. Perhaps the most succinct statement of the doctrine in Scripture is found in Ephesians 1:11, which speaks of God 'who works all things after the counsel of his will'. Paul makes the same point in a more intimate context in Romans 8:28: 'We know that God causes all things to work together for good to those who love God, to those who are called according to his purpose.'

Theistic evolution 'majors' on the providence of God, since it claims that God used providence to bring about the created order. That is, he used the natural processes of evolution to achieve creation and continues to uphold the cosmos by those same processes. This, claim theistic evolutionists, provides an elegant concept of the relationship between God and his universe. He works only through natural law and thus *all events* are the works of God in this sense. This obviously gives rise to the strongest possible doctrine of providence, they claim.

However, this position is not as strong as it might appear at first sight. For what it actually does is create a kind of barrier between God and the physical universe. It begins with the statement that God created the laws of nature: he made this world to function in the way that it does and the laws of nature then determine what happens in the cosmos. *God is obliged to operate on the physical world through the interface of natural law.* He cannot get around this. He has to work through this agency of natural process and cannot interact directly or independently with the physical world.

Now this creates all kinds of difficulty, because the theistic evolutionist, if he believes the Bible, must also believe in miracles. He must believe in the original *ex nihilo* creation, the resurrection of Christ and all the other Bible miracles. So, logically at least, he has an uneasy mind. Since he claims that God only interacts with the physical world via the interface of natural law, all miracles must ultimately be explained in terms of such law. In other words, there are no such things as miracles!

In reply to this it might be argued that there is no claim in Scripture that 'miracles' do actually violate natural law. Their precise nature is not discussed in the Bible, which is far more concerned with their effects (evoking wonder, serving as signs and glorifying God). There are also definite cases where natural causes are given, as in the Red Sea crossing, where the agency of a strong wind was employed to effect the 'miracle' in question. Is it not possible, then, that all miracles are similarly explicable in natural terms and that their value lay in the subjective impressions made upon those who looked on?

This, however, comes perilously close to accusing God of performing conjuring tricks to deceive the people. If water was turned to wine at Christ's command by natural process, those who observed the miracle were certainly not aware of this fact. Otherwise they would not have believed in him on account of the signs he performed. The whole purpose of such signs was to demonstrate that Christ possessed powers over the material world that could only come from God. 'No one can do these signs that you do unless God is with him,' declares Nicodemus in John 3:2. This can only mean that Christ could interrupt, alter or accelerate natural processes. Whatever else this means, it certainly shows that the events in question were not the outcome of unchanged natural law. Let us take as an example the raising of the dead. It is not beyond the bounds of possibility that medical science will one day be able to reverse the process of death by regenerative techniques and bring back to life those who have been 'dead' for hours or even days. If that ever occurs it will be by natural process and not by changes in the laws of nature. Might this not indicate that Christ's miracles of resurrecting the dead were achieved by natural means as yet unknown to us? The answer must surely be negative. For Christ achieved these results *without means*, apart from his command. *To raise the dead without means* implies nothing but the reversal of natural process, a genuine miracle that demands the alteration of natural law.

The attempt to limit God so that he operates on the physical world only through the agency of natural law is part of a wider characteristic of theistic evolution, namely its tendency to separate spiritual events from physical ones. There is a strong dichotomy between the physical and the spiritual in the thinking of theistic evolutionists which leads to a kind of evangelical deism. God is near spiritually but distant physically. The doctrine of the immanence of God is implicitly denied, or at least ignored. The sense of proximity invoked by such scriptures as 'In him we live and move and have our being' (Acts 17:28 AV) is greatly weakened. The idea that God opens his hand and satisfies the desire of every living thing (Ps. 145:16) is reduced to mere poetry.

The immediacy of God is abandoned.

Creationism offers a much stronger doctrine of God's interaction with the physical universe and man himself. Creationism recognizes, of course, the centrality of providence. Its position on this subject is just as positive as that of theistic evolution. Equally, God's spiritual activity among men is a matter of agreement between creationists and theistic evolutionists. But creationism also makes room for God to interact with the world by miraculous means in which the laws of nature as we know them are set aside. Furthermore (and this is important), these three modes of activity are not independent or in conflict, but represent three aspects of the same activity of God. He works in providence, miracle and spirit, but the work is one and the purpose is one. What is this single process of divine interaction with the cosmos?

Two verses of Scripture provide the essential answer to this question. We read in Colossians 1:17 that in Christ 'all things hold together' (cohere, consist). The integrity of all things is established and maintained through Christ. We shall not develop the Christocentric significance of this statement here, for this is discussed exhaustively in chapter 7. We simply notice now that the entire universe, physical and spiritual, coheres in God. In the preceding verse Paul makes explicit reference to both the material universe and the spiritual powers. All, avers the apostle, have been created through Christ and for him. And all, equally, derive their continuing existence from him.

Similarly, in Hebrews 1:3 we are told that the 'word of [Christ's] power' upholds all things. In so far as this includes the physical universe we may equate the 'word of his power' with natural law, for in scientific terms it is the latter which upholds the cosmos. More accurately we should perhaps say that the word of God's power equates to those principles that we seek, imperfectly, to represent by our 'laws of nature'.

But the word of God's power is not *limited* to natural law. There is the angelic creation, for example, which is not governed by natural process. 'All things' is an extremely comprehensive term. It comprehends not only the material cosmos but also the angelic realm, principalities and powers, heaven and hell, the timelessness of eternity and possibly other things that we cannot even conceive. All of these are upheld by the same divine logos.

Notice the essential unity of God's working. There is no 'trichotomy' here, as if he worked differently in providence, miracle and grace. The *same* word upholds all the realms of God's dominion, simultaneously and harmoniously, so that spiritual purposes are worked out in material events and physical manifestations point us to spiritual realities (Ps. 19; Rom. 1).

Notice also the use of the present tense in these statements in Colossians and Hebrews. The relationship between God and the universe is characterized by a perpetual 'now'. If, hypothetically, God were to cease to exist, the entirety of all things other than God would instantly suffer the same fate. This is not to equate God with nature; that would be pantheism. But equally, we must not divorce God from nature, for that is deism. We have to recognize that God is immanent. We exist, the universe exists and the spiritual world exists, because God exists and wills all things to function, moment by moment, in accordance with 'the counsel of his will' (Eph. 1:11).

It is this relationship between the living God and the created order that lies at the heart of creationism. For when seen from this viewpoint, providence (and the natural law by which it operates) and miracle are alike the expressed intent of God. If natural process is the moment-by-moment consequence of God's commands, then deviations from such process (miracles) are of the same essence and should excite no special concern. It is only if we impose upon natural law some self-existence independent of God, that we create conceptual problems for ourselves in understanding the miraculous. Needless to say, such a self-existent view of nature is the essence of deism.

Just as natural law and miracle can be unified by this theology, so also can God's dealings with the material and spiritual realms be brought together. We have already noticed how, in Colossians 1:16,17, these realms are not distinguished from each other in respect of their creation, purpose and integrity. We find the same unity implicit in Hebrews 1:1–3, where the material creation and its sustenance are mentioned in the same breath as the spiritual revelation of God in Christ. The word of his power upholds the realms of nature and heaven in a single operation of the power of God. It is only our mental limitation that causes us to divorce the material from the spiritual in the way that we do. God sees things differently. To us, for example, the biblical concept of a 'spiritual body', discussed in 1 Corinthians 15:35-58 seems strange. How can a 'body', with its undoubted material and corporeal nature be, at the same time, a spiritual entity? Yet this is clearly the case with the resurrection body. The problem lies entirely in our reluctance to adopt a unified view of the dominion of God, in an unscriptural distinction between the physical and spiritual realms.

Implicit in theistic evolution is the tendency to imprison God within the spiritual realm, to separate him from the physical world behind a barrier of natural law. By contrast, creationism sees a totally unrestricted Deity, who orders all things after the counsel of his will, in heaven and earth alike. Emphasizing the immediacy of God, it gives an almost frightening view of his power as he holds 'the life of every living thing' in his hands (Job 12:10). Every blink of our eyelids, every pulse of our hearts, is willed by God. Our total dependence upon God is brought home to us, as is our responsibility to worship him as God. He is very near, frighteningly near. Yet to those who know him, this is a matter for rejoicing and confidence, as well as godly fear.

It is surely not a matter of indifference whether we believe in creationism or theistic evolution.

6.
The cosmos – a biblical perspective

So far we have been concerned mainly with an evaluation of the claims of evolutionists in the light of biblical teaching. We now turn our attention to those who adopt the creationist view and to the tendency for 'scientific creationism' to replace 'biblical creationism' as the predominant emphasis in their thinking. Rightly defined, scientific creationism has an important role, but for the Christian it must always take second place to biblical revelation. In this chapter we see how the biblical view of origins differs from any purely scientific concept of 'creation'.

The emergence of scientific creationism

It might be appropriate to introduce my subject by reviewing briefly the progress of the creationist movement world-wide. As we look back over the last few years we can see that there has been a remarkable growth in interest in the subject of creation. The creationist movement, viewed as a world-wide phenomenon, exhibits much evidence of growth. This development is apparent, both in the rise of creationist groups in different nations, and in the attention being given to what they have to say. Creationism is not confined to the U.S.A., as some commentators seem to think. In European countries strong movements have been formed in Sweden, Holland and Germany, while the growth of creationism in Eastern lands is also evident. Australia affords another excellent example, where the creationist journal *Ex Nihilo* is published. Thus we can be encouraged by the rise of these groups where previously, as far as we know, there was no united testimony to the

Christian and biblical position on creation.

Not only has growth occurred in the establishment of groups in different countries, but also in what I might call the credibility of the creationist position. Over recent months and years we have seen an increasing willingness on the part of the mass media at least to air the views and opinions of creationists. Organs like the BBC, of course, still exhibit an almost total bias towards the evolutionary perspective, but nevertheless they have been willing to do what in earlier years they refused to do, namely, to allow creationists time and exposure in the media to promote, or at least express, their views.

There has also been an increase in public awareness, perhaps linked to what I have just said, and a corresponding increase in opposition and reaction by the evolutionary establishment. I read just the other day that a recent Gallup poll in the U.S.A. came up with the startling result that 44 per cent of all Americans actually preferred to believe in a recent miraculous creation than in evolution, and that a further 38 per cent were believers in creation by a process of theistic evolution. I do not know how accurate Mr Gallup's figures are in this particular case. I make frequent visits to the other side of the Atlantic and would not have thought that nearly half the population there were believers in special creation. But it does indicate that the public awareness and acceptability of creationism has undergone a great advance.

The reaction is becoming increasingly shrill. The evolutionary camp is becoming more and more intolerant. In Britain, a spate of correspondence in *The Times* during 1982 exhibited a growing concern and fear among the evolutionary establishment that creationist views might become established and accepted.

But there is also growth in another area, one which I consider particularly important and which is highly relevant to what I have to say in this chapter. There has been a growth in Christian awareness of the importance of the doctrine of creation. It wasn't long ago that a reviewer of one of my books took me to task for saying that we need a theology of science in order to evangelize effectively in our modern society. He said we must preach the gospel and this creation business ought to be kept as a secondary activity, a kind of hobby, as it were. But I cannot see it that way. I believe the doctrine of creation is absolutely fundamental to a biblical understanding of the nature of God. If you ask the Scriptures, particularly the Old Testament, what kind of a god is God, the

answer you will get is that he is the one who created the heavens
and the earth. That is God's 'trademark', his major identification.
We find this emphasis throughout the pages of the Old Testament, but not only there. When the apostle Paul on his missionary
journeys encountered untaught groups of people, as in Lystra and
Derbe, he was at pains to identify the God and Father of our Lord
Jesus Christ as the one who created the heavens and the earth.
Without a full-blooded doctrine of creation, even our gospel
preaching is emasculated and weak. I do not think it is any acci-
dent that John, as he sets out in his Gospel to present the Lord
Jesus Christ, begins by identifying Christ as the 'Logos' who
made all things. I therefore welcome the growing awareness that
the doctrine of creation is a vital and essential part of the entire
Christian message and that without it we have a weakened gospel.

But at the same time there is a growing problem that I discern
and which I shall use to introduce a number of positive statements
that will follow. The problem is a growing divorce between what
we might call 'scientific creationism' and biblical creationism.
The distinction I am making arises largely from the problems that
our American brethren face concerning the teaching of creation
and evolution in their state schools. The problem is that under the
American Constitution, it is not permissible to teach religion or
sectarianism in the state schools. The American branch of the
creationist movement has therefore attempted to develop a scientific creationism that has no religious content. They present the
scientific evidence and observations relating to the universe and to
life as things that can best be interpreted in terms of a creation
model. That is, they take scientific evidence from all branches of
science and instead of interpreting that evidence, as most people
do, in terms of an evolutionary model, they fit it instead to a
creationist scenario. They examine the evidence and say, 'As we
look at the details we see that they are more consistent with a recent creation than with a process of evolution over billions of
years.' They are attempting to eliminate the religious element
from the creationist position. Thus in a recent test case in Arkan-
sas, it was argued that creationism could properly be taught
alongside evolution in schools, because they were both scientific
models, alternative scientific models, and that creationism was
just as free of religious content as was evolution. The argument
was thrown out in that particular case, but there will no doubt be
other such cases.

Much as one can understand the particular reasons for its adoption in the U.S.A., scientific creationism, does, it seems to me, involve a number of very real dangers and problems. First of all, of course, it is quite obvious that one can join forces in scientific creationism with all kinds of non-Christian beliefs and outlooks. There are Buddhists who are scientific creationists. There are Jehovah's Witnesses who are scientific creationists. There are even those who make no religious profession at all who are scientific creationists. An example of this is the book *Evolution from Space* published by Sir Fred Hoyle and Chandra Wickramasinghe, which is both entertaining and informative, and I would recommend it as interesting reading. They have a concluding chapter entitled 'Convergence to God', and they reason from the scientific evidence to a position where they state that the information content of living things could not possibly have arisen by chance and must therefore be the product of intelligence. They are at pains to point out, however, that their god, their ultimate intelligence, bears no relation to the gods of conventional religions and least of all to the God of Christianity. So, scientific creationism is a-Christian, if I can coin that expression. It is not anti-Christian, of course, but it is a-Christian. It is devoid of a Christian content and quite deliberately so. People may say, of course, that this is quite all right, because it simply represents a step in the right direction. If we can convince men that it is reasonable and rational to believe in creation on the grounds of scientific evidence, we can at a later stage impress upon them the truth of the Christian revelation. This argument has some strength, and I have used it myself. But more recently I have begun to wonder whether that is as true as might appear at first sight. I wonder if there is not in scientific creationism a danger of replacing one false god with another — of replacing the false god of evolution by a false god of deism. For scientific creationism, if it leads anywhere in a religious sense, leads to deism and not to Christian faith.

In what ways does the god with whom one comes up by reasoning from scientific creationism differ from the God of biblical revelation? Well, I would suggest one or two very important ways. If we turn to Hebrews 11:3, we read as follows: 'By faith we understand that the worlds were prepared (or "framed" as the Authorized Version has it) by the word of God, so that what is seen was not made out of things which are visible.' This verse is normally regarded as a statement of creation *ex nihilo*, that God created the physical and material universe out of nothing. I believe that is a proper interpretation of the verse, but the thing I want to emphasize is the statement that it is 'by faith' that we understand that the worlds were framed by the Word of God. It is by faith that we arrive at this conclusion, not by rational argument or deduction. I am well aware that Romans 1 suggests that man ought to be able to deduce true facts about God by observation of the cosmos. But the whole point of Romans 1 is to state that man *fails* to do that and Hebrews tells us plainly that a true view of the God of creation is to be obtained through faith and faith alone. Therefore by definition the god whose existence and activity we may deduce on the basis of scientific creationism, the prime cause of all things at whom we might arrive by examination of the scientific evidence, cannot be the God of revelation, because we are told on the authority of Scripture that he is recognized by faith and not by argument.

I think one can go on to generalize the point a little and suggest that the person who begins with scientific creationism and argues his way through to the existence of a creator, having achieved that degree of understanding by his own unaided reasoning, is *less* likely to recognize the importance of revelation to provide a further, deeper and more extensive knowledge of God. Therefore, I have this concern that, while I clearly recognize the reasons for and the purpose of scientific creationism, it might well lead men to a god who is not the God of biblical revelation, to a god of man's own construction, to a deistic god who can be known other than by faith.

I am not trying to be contentious. I am simply pointing out the dangers in this growing emphasis on scientific creationism and I think that we have to be very careful indeed before we go too far down that road. There are dangers that have to be avoided. There is infinitely more about the God of creation than can be revealed or even hinted at by scientific creationism. I believe it is our task to present a biblical world-view, a view of creation which begins with revelation rather than with our own unaided reasoning. A biblical world-view will present the true God and not a deistic creator.

This, in essence, is the purpose of this chapter. I want us to look at the cosmos through the eyes of Scripture. I want us to adopt a biblical perspective on the cosmos. I want us to move away from a scientific creationist position to a truly biblical creationist position and to point the way by which we can avoid the pitfalls implicit in scientific creationism and provide a full and faithful picture of the cosmos and its Creator.

We shall look first of all at the *unity* of the cosmos, secondly at its *destiny* and thirdly at its *design*. We shall see how the Bible points us to a full and proper understanding of the cosmos under these three categories. In each case we are going to look first at the testimony of science and then at the testimony of Scripture, so that we can see the parallels and the differences that emerge.

The cosmos – its unity

Let us begin by noting that the word 'cosmos' means an arrangement. It means an arrangement of beauty – that is the basic meaning of the word. It has links with the word 'cosmetic' and comes from a Greek verb which means to beautify, adorn or set in order. The cosmos, by definition, means an arrangement, an ordered system. The name itself, therefore, implies that the universe, in so far as we describe it as a cosmos, is an integrated and harmonious whole – a unity. And, of course, the word 'universe' is simply the Latin equivalent of 'cosmos' in that sense.

What do we mean by the unity of the cosmos? Look first at the testimony of science itself. Science takes us quite a long way in considering the cosmos as a unity, an integrated and harmonious system. First of all, we have the testimony of science with regard to the *uniformity* or consistency of scientific law both in space and in time. This is both a result of scientific investigation and a basic axiom of scientific method. It is a result of scientific investigation in the sense that, as far as it has been tested, the proposal has been demonstrated to be sound. The laws of science are the same wherever they are tested, wherever they are investigated and whenever they are subjected to those tests. Science, therefore, demonstrates that the laws of science are consistent. They do not change from one day to another, from one century to the next. They do not change from one place to another upon the face of earth, nor indeed, as far as we know, do they change in their nature from one part of the universe to another. At the same time, of course, science cannot actually prove the uniformity of scientific law. All it can say is that it has not so far found any exception to that uniformity. Thus science proceeds upon the assumption that scientific law is uniform and unchangeable both in space and in time.

That is, perhaps, self-evident, something that scientists simply take for granted and the rest of us would hardly want to question anyway. But when we stop to think about it, we realize that it is by no means self-evident that this should be so. Why should the law of gravity be the same in some distant galaxy as it is here upon earth? Why should the laws that control the behaviour of light and radiation be the same in all parts of the universe and at all times? Surely the unified character of the entire universal system must have profound implications. Others have given critiques of the 'big bang' theory of the origin and evolution of the universe. In that theory, we have a good example of the scientist's desire to unify his description of the universe, to present it as a unity, as the product of a single unique event and not that of a number of quite different origination events which might have given rise to a variation of scientific law from place to place within the universe. There is an implication therefore in science, both in its axioms and in its findings, that the cosmos is a unity, because the same laws control its activity and interactions throughout all time. If this were not so it would be very difficult indeed to carry on the business that we describe as science.

Not only, however, do we have the concept of the uniformity of law in time and space, we have the concept of *system*. What do I mean by that? I mean that the universe is not made up of a vast number of independently acting entities or bodies, or fields or whatever you might like to specify. Things work together in the universe; there is interaction. What do we mean by a system? The word 'system' describes a situation in which a number of different or independent entities work together to cause effects that could not be produced by those entities independently. We are familiar with the concept of system. We talk about the solar system, where the planets and the sun interact to produce a working cosmological machine. We talk about ecological systems in which different forms of life co-exist in a harmonious balance and equilibrium. We talk about weather systems, we talk about biological systems. We talk about the endocrine system, for example, in the body, where we have different glands producing different substances but somehow all working together to produce a balance which controls the health and life of the individual. We talk about systems when we discuss nuclear structure. Wherever we look in the universe, things do not go their own sweet way. Things are interacting, working together, conspiring together, one might almost say, to produce effects which are the results of systematic operation. This also testifies within the body of science to the unity or compatibility of the different concepts, laws and bodies that make up the universe.

Thirdly, there is the concept of *economy*. Science tells us that the universe is economic. What do I mean by that? I can best explain it by way of example, namely that the infinite variety of chemical substances and materials, whether living or non-living, that make up this universe, are all constructed from fewer than one hundred naturally occurring elements. Here is an economy. Fewer than a hundred elements are sufficient to produce the millions of different substances, objects and bodies that we observe in the universe. The use of a few basic building blocks to construct a vast variety of objects and systems is the essence of economy. Another example is the common chemistry of life. From no more than four relatively simple molecules, built into the larger DNA molecule, the entire biosphere can be constructed with all its infinite variety. It is like using an alphabet of just four letters to construct a code by which an infinite variety of different messages can be conveyed. This 'genetic code' controls the form and function of all living creatures and gives rise to the vast variety that we recognize within the biological world.

Economy points to the basic unity of the cosmos. The principle of economy points to the fact that all the myriad diverse manifestations of life and of inanimate matter, the entire universe is actually constructed both physically and conceptually from a very small number of basic building blocks. To some extent one can define science as the process of reducing this very complicated world in which we live (and the vast range of systems, interactions and substances that we observe) to a few simple laws and principles.

This is the philosopher's stone, if you like, for which the scientist is seeking — the universal law, the universal principle, from which everything else that happens can be derived as a special case or application. This is what drives the pure scientist, at least, in his search for simplicity in the midst of complexity. So, then, the testimony of science to the unity of the cosmos is considerable and extensive. But let us move on to the testimony of Scripture in this regard.

Scripture agrees with science, very largely. Scripture says, 'Yes, all that we find concerning the unity of the cosmos in science is to be expected.' But Scripture traces that unity back to a far more fundamental cause. Scripture speaks first of all of a common origin of all things. It tells us that God in the beginning created the heavens and the earth. It tells us, in the words of the opening chapter of John's Gospel, that all things were made by him and then it repeats the same thing in a negative fashion: 'Apart from him nothing came into being that has come into being.' John is concerned to impress upon us that God (and he is speaking particularly of Christ, as we shall see in a moment) is the sole origin of all things, whether they be visible or invisible, spiritual or material. God is the common source and originator of all things. He did not take some pre-existing substance and transform it into the world. This is the whole thrust of the doctrine of *ex nihilo* creation. He created this entire universe from pure spirit, from pure thought, from pure mind. Therefore we expect the cosmos to be a unity, to have common and universal laws. We expect the things that science turns up in its progress; we expect there to be some simple, unifying principle that lies behind the entire universe. This principle, for which science seeks, is in fact revealed in Scripture. It is the principle that all things came from the mind of God.

Scripture speaks not only of a common origin of all things, but of a common source of all existence. One of the major teachings of the Bible is that God not only created all things, but also sustains all things. For the present we will illustrate this by looking at two verses, one in Hebrews 1 and one in Colossians 1. In Colossians 1:17 we read of Christ that 'He is before all things, and in him all things hold together [or consist].' It is evident from the context that 'all things' here include the entire physical universe. And if this verse in Colossians were not enough, Hebrews goes on to say that Christ 'upholds all things by the word of his power'. Thus we have a present-tense sustenance of the universe; so much so, that the very laws of science viewed in the biblical perspective are the thoughts of God. The laws of science are the word of God's power, by which he upholds the entire physical and natural universe. That is the only interpretation that one can place upon those verses.

But in Scripture not only do we have a common origin of all things and a common source of all existence, but we also have a common *ground* of all existence. I am differentiating here between a *source* and a *ground* (for want of better words perhaps). In order to establish what I mean by a common ground of all existence I would turn our attention to the verse in Colossians that precedes the one we have just looked at. Here we read, 'He [Christ] is the image of the invisible God, the first-born of all creation. For in him all things were created, both in the heavens and on earth, visible and invisible, whether thrones or dominions or rulers or authorities – all things have been created through him and for him. And he is before all things, and in him all things hold together.' We notice that there are three prepositions involved. All things were created *in* him, *through* him and *for* him. While, therefore, we can speak from Colossians 1:17 of Christ being the source of all existence, in that he upholds all things moment by moment by the word of his power, the Scripture goes beyond that. It really says that you cannot think of the created order without Christ. Christ, as it were, surrounds the cosmos. For the cosmos was created *in* him, *through* him and *for* him. I do not have space here to work out in detail precisely what those separate statements mean. I just want to point out that they add up to a Christocentric (Christ-centred) cosmos. It is not simply that Christ created; it is not simply that Christ sustains. It is that the cosmos only has existence, meaning, significance and purpose in terms of Christ – in him, through him, for him. I believe that this is perhaps the central point of what I have to say. We cannot have a truly biblical perspective on the cosmos without recognizing the absolute centrality of Christ.

It is normal for us to think in terms of God the Creator. We may even degenerate, as I said earlier, to a deistic position arrived at by our deductions from science and our human observations. But even as Christians we often think separately of God as the Creator and Christ as the Saviour. That is quite wrong. We must understand that a fully biblical view of the cosmos is a Christ-centred view. What we are being told here in Colossians, and elsewhere, is that we cannot understand the cosmos, we cannot fully comprehend the universe in which we live unless we relate that universe to Christ, for it was created in him, through him and for him.

It is this Christocentric creationism that sets the biblical revelation apart from all other creationist positions and theories. It seems to me that our task, as Christians, is to present Christ as the Christ of the cosmos and to present the cosmos as the cosmos of

Christ. The next and final chapter of this book will develop this theme further.

The cosmos – its destiny

What is the destiny of the cosmos? Here also science has its testimony and I am going to deal with this fairly briefly. It is quite clear that science implicitly accepts or teaches that there is a destiny for the cosmos. The very nature of time indicates that there is a destiny, that the cosmos is moving onwards to some future condition, state or consummation that science tries to predict in a variety of ways. The 'arrow' of time (the fact that we cannot go backwards and forwards in time as we can go backwards and forwards in space) constitutes a problem which has greatly exercised scientists and philosophers. The very fact of time, therefore, means that we are moving inexorably on towards a future destiny. Of course, the scientific scenarios of that destiny differ considerably. There are those who talk about a heat death in which the earth will be swallowed up by an expanding sun. Others speak of the entropy death, which is the total decay of all things into universal randomness; time will cease and there will be no further change or movement. In yet another type of scenario one looks forward down the arrow of time with the optimism of the evolutionist, who believes that evolution will carry mankind and the world forward to greater and greater things. But one point is clear: science, by the nature of time, indicates that there *is* destiny. I suppose it could also be said that the nature of science itself, with its application in future technology, also implies a destiny, and one that varies between the hope of advancement in medical science and the fears of nuclear war and ecological disaster. Whatever scenario we adopt, we are saying that science, its growth and its application, is going to lead us somewhere, although we don't know where. That 'somewhere' may be future triumph, it may be future disaster, but we can do little about it.

The nature of man also implies destiny. The nature of time, the nature of science and the nature of man all point to a destiny. Man has an inbuilt urge to self-improvement. Whether it be on the technical, social, political or personal level, man is always looking forward to a better future, always striving for improvement. It seems to be innate within the human breast to seek a destiny.

As we look around therefore, even with our unaided senses, we see that the cosmos is going somewhere. It is moving forward; it cannot go back, it cannot stand still. There is therefore by definition a destiny that awaits us. But that destiny is unclear.

The testimony of Scripture is totally different from the scenarios of science. The first thing I notice as I read my Bible is that the destiny of the cosmos, of the material creation, is bound up with the destiny of man, and in particular with the destiny of the church. This is an interesting fact, because we normally tend to separate the material world from the spiritual world. We tend to put them in different categories. We think of the material world as having no particular influence or impact upon the spiritual world and we think of the spiritual realm as having no particular relevance to the material. But that is not the teaching of the New Testament. If we turn to Romans 8, for example, we read words like this: 'The anxious longing of the creation waits eagerly for the revealing of the sons of God. For the creation was subjected to futility, not of its own will, but because of him who subjected it, in hope that the creation itself also will be set free from its slavery to corruption into the freedom of the glory of the children of God. For we know that the whole creation groans and suffers the pains of childbirth together until now. And not only this, but also we ourselves groan within ourselves, waiting eagerly for our adoption . . . the redemption of the body.'

The apostle Paul here ties together the future destiny of the cosmos, the physical universe, and the future destiny of the church. We cannot here look into the question of the subjection of the universe to vanity or futility. One may construe this subjection as the effect of the fall of man, so that even from the earliest date the physical universe is linked together with the fate and behaviour of man. Regardless of this, however, it is quite clear that the *future* destiny of the cosmos is bound up in Christian revelation with the future destiny of the church of Jesus Christ. We might move on to Revelation and to 2 Peter to read about the new heaven and the new earth which we can no doubt equate with the transformation that Paul describes in Romans 8. In 2 Peter 3, there is a long passage on the future of the universe. He speaks of the present heavens and earth being reserved for fire, kept for the day of judgement and destruction, not of the universe, but of 'ungodly men'. Then he goes on to say that there will be a new heaven and a new earth. He says, ['We look for and hasten] the coming of the day of God, on account of which the heavens will be destroyed by burning, and the elements will melt with intense heat. But according to his promise' (and he refers back here to the prophet Isaiah) 'we are looking for new heavens and a new earth, in which righteousness dwells.' Now we cannot spiritualize away these references because they plainly refer to the physical cosmos in which we live. We cannot, perhaps, speculate too far on the nature and character of the new heavens and the new earth which will replace the present physical order. We are told that there will be no more unrighteousness; we are told in Romans 8 that the universe will be delivered from its slavery to corruption; but just what this will mean in terms of a different kind of physical universe we do not know. But it is fairly clear to me that the New Testament writers are not simply speaking of a restoration of the universe that existed before the fall of Adam, because we also read of the resurrection of the physical body. In 1 Corinthians we read that the body is sown a physical body, but raised a spiritual body. It seems to me, therefore, that the new heavens and the new earth will be an order in which that which is spiritual and that which is physical and material will be brought together into an even greater cosmological unity than we observe today. This is also suggested by Ephesians 1:9,10, where again we find a Christological emphasis. We read, '[God] made known to us the mystery of his will, according to his kind intention which he purposed in him [Christ] with a view to an administration [a future state of affairs] suitable to the fulness of the times.' What is this 'administration' to be? It is to be 'the summing up of all things in Christ, things in the heavens and things upon the earth'. There is to be a destiny involving the physical universe, the new heavens, the new earth, in a new level of integration between the physical and the spiritual. But, additionally, all this is to be in Christ. All things in heaven and earth, which quite plainly include the physical universe, are to be 'summed up in him'. Once again we see a Christocentricity which characterizes and marks out the biblical testimony to the nature and history of the cosmos.

The cosmos – its design

The idea of design in nature is perhaps thought rather old-fashioned. We may think of Paley's watchmaker and consider that the idea and concept of design went out round about his time. Nevertheless, the whole concept of design in the cosmos is something that deserves a new look, a new investigation. For one thing, although science does not acknowledge design as such in the universe, it nevertheless recognizes a number of the essential ingredients of design. It recognizes *order*, for example, and that order in nature is the rule rather than the exception. Order is more common than disorder. I can give an example from my own discipline of materials science. The vast majority of the substances and materials that we find naturally, or manufacture artificially, are crystalline. There are a few which are amorphous and do not possess order, but the majority of solid substances are crystalline. Wherever you look in the universe you find order and systematic arrangement. This is one of the characteristics of design. Then, again, science recognizes *information*. It recognizes the existence of a genetic code, for example, in which information is stored. Information is another essential ingredient of design. Science also admits that many of the structures and systems in this world appear to have been brought into being to serve a *purpose*, which, of course, on a purely evolutionary view cannot be admitted. But there is a great dilemma in the self-imposed materialism of science which says we cannot consider and will not consider anything teleological in nature. The dilemma is that the laws of science which explain the order and the information that are found in nature cannot themselves be explained by science. The existence of those laws has to be taken simply as axiomatic, something given, something that science itself cannot explain. So science points towards the concept of design in the cosmos, although it is too shy to use the word explicitly.

But what of the testimony of Scripture? Well here, I believe, we have a very plain statement. First of all, let me define what I mean by design. By design I mean fitness for a purpose. In common usage we use the word 'design' to signify two different things. One use is to describe something which is aesthetically pleasing. We say that an object is well designed, if it is visually attractive. But then, if we are engineers or have any connection with that profession, we use the word 'design' in a rather more technical sense, meaning 'fitness for purpose'. A thing is designed in order to fulfil a function. Indeed, the second definition is capable of embracing the aesthetic definition, if the purpose of the object or system in question is to give aesthetic pleasure. So design is fitness for purpose. Design is that attribute (of an object or a system) of being suited to a purpose. It is interesting that the concept of fitness for purpose is superficially similar to the evolutionary concept of adaptation. This expression describes, in particular, an ability to survive in a given environment. But the concept of adaptation falls far short of our definition of design. Let me give just one example of why I can say that.

Fitness for purpose is what we mean by design. Adaptation means fitness for survival. So evolutionary adaptation can only conceive *purpose* in terms of *survival*. To survive is the only purpose of existence. That has to be the limit to which evolutionary thinking can take us. But if the only purpose in life is to survive, then it is very difficult to see how evolution has happened at all, because the amoeba is perfectly adapted for survival. Why then did it, or something like it, need to evolve into the vast diversity of living forms that we know today? There is a real philosophical *impasse* for the theory of evolution, as it seeks to define what it means by adaptation.

The biblical declaration of design goes infinitely further. We can talk about purpose in biblical terms in a way that we cannot possibly discuss in terms of evolution. Therefore, because we can talk about purpose, we can talk about design.

Now, you may ask, where does the Bible declare the principles of design in the cosmos? Well, there are many scriptures that point in this direction, but I am going to be satisfied with only one, and that is to be found in the opening chapter of the Bible, in Genesis 1. There is a refrain that occurs throughout that chapter, the meaning of which is, I think, very often forgotten or unrecognized. That refrain is the statement that God looked at the things that he had made and pronounced them 'good'. The statement is made on day 1 of the creation record, it is made twice on day 3, once each on days 4 and 5, and twice again on day 6. So it is a genuine refrain that runs throughout the creation narrative. Seven times we read that God looked at what he had made and 'it was good'. In the closing verse we are told: 'It was very good.' Now I don't know what you understand by those words, but to me they are a very plain statement on the design of the cosmos. For you cannot interpret the word 'good' in a *moral* sense in that chapter, because many of the things that are described as good are inanimate, material objects. They were the result of God's creative acts, with no morality involved. So 'good' cannot be used there in the moral sense of good as opposed to evil. It must therefore be used in the sense of 'fitness for purpose'. When God pronounced that that which he had made was good, he could only have meant that it was suited perfectly and totally for the purpose he had in mind when he made it. It seems to me therefore that the refrain in Genesis 1 is the plainest possible statement that the cosmos was subject to design.

This brings us to our last point, namely, what *was* God's purpose? Accepting that the cosmos was designed, was fitted for a purpose, then what was that purpose? The purpose is very clearly revealed in Scripture. It is that all things should subserve the glory of God, We may go back to Psalm 19 and read there that

The heavens are telling of the glory of God;
and their expanse is declaring the work of his hands.
Day to day pours forth speech,
and night to night reveals knowledge.

The creation, the cosmos, reveals and declares the glory of God. We read similar words, less poetic perhaps, in the first chapter of Romans. We could show from one scripture and another that the whole purpose of the cosmos is to demonstrate the glory of God and, in particular, certain aspects of that glory. It reveals his power, it reveals his Godhead, it reveals his perfection. It reveals his tenderness and his care, his innate beauty, his rationality. It reveals his faithfulness. I have no doubt that, with a little extra thought, one could easily add to that list.

Here, then, is the purpose of the cosmos: to subserve and to proclaim, to identify and to reveal the glory of God in its manifold aspects. The design of the cosmos resides in its fitness for that purpose. The Scripture, both in Old and New Testaments, can say that the cosmos is perfectly designed, perfectly fitted to reveal and to proclaim the glory of God.

But, finally, let us remind ourselves that even the design of the cosmos is Christ-centred. In Ephesians 1:10 we read that the cosmos was something that God purposed *in Christ*, and in Colossians 1:16 that all things were created *for him*. Let us therefore return to the Christ-centredness and Christ-relatedness of the biblical perspective on the cosmos. We should be satisfied with nothing less.

7.
Christe and the cosmos

In this final chapter we develop in much greater detail the concept with which we closed the previous chapter, namely, the centrality of Christ to any correct view of the universe. Taking Colossians 1 as our starting-point, we shall see how the Bible relates all things to Christ, whether in the material creation or the spiritual domain. In turn, Christ is presented as the 'image of the invisible God', so that Creator and creation are brought together in him. In particular, the purpose of the physical cosmos is seen to relate to the calling, salvation and glorification of the church, the body of Christ.

Setting the scene

The matters we are about to discuss come closer to the heart of creationism than any other topics treated in this book. Yet, strangely, they have received scant attention in the current debate on evolution and creation. Our thinking will be based on a passage from chapter 1 of Colossians, beginning in verse 13: 'For [God] delivered us from the domain of darkness, and transferred us to the kingdom of his beloved Son, in whom we have redemption, the forgiveness of sins. And he is the image of the invisible God, the firstborn of all creation. For in him all things were created, both in the heavens and on the earth, visible and invisible, whether thrones or dominions or rulers or authorities – all things have been created through him and for him. And he is before all things, and in him all things hold together. He is also head of the body, the church; and he is the beginning, the first-born from the dead; so that he himself might come to have first place in everything. For it was the Father's good pleasure for all the fulness to dwell in him, and through him to reconcile all things to himself, having made peace through the blood of his cross; through him, I say, whether things on earth or things in heaven.'

In this passage, which, of course, is one of the great Christological passages of the New Testament, we see three things in regard to the person of Christ. We see first of all *his relationship to God the Father*. We see secondly *his relationship to the cosmos, the created order*. Thirdly we see *his relationship to the church*. In this chapter we are going to explore these three relationships, or better, this threefold relationship. For although our point of interest is Christ and the cosmos, it would be a mistake to isolate this one relationship and ignore the others. For what Paul does here is, quite deliberately, to link these three things together. He begins with the triune God, moves on to consider Christ and the physical universe and then ends with a dissertation on Christ and the church. These three relationships are, in fact, a unity. Christ's relationship to the created order cannot be understood without reference to his relationship to God and the church.

The invisibility of God

Let us begin in verse 15 and consider what we are told here about Christ and God. We read, 'He is the image of the invisible God.' There are many things we could say about the doctrine of the Trinity, but that is not my present purpose. I want rather to concentrate on the particular significance of these words. What does it mean that Christ is the 'image of God'?

The first thing we notice is that God is *invisible*. God cannot be seen, cannot be discerned, cannot be comprehended by unaided human faculties. The invisibility of God is not a reference solely to his incorporeal nature, to the fact that God is spirit, so that we cannot see him with our physical eyes. Rather, in consonance with the entire teaching of Scripture, it speaks of the unapproachability of God. Of course, these words do include the fact that God is spirit, but they also signify that he is holy. Remember how in Exodus 33:18 Moses makes his great request to God: 'I pray thee, show me thy glory!' The awe-inspiring reply that he received was definitive of the holiness of God: 'No man can see me and live.'

God is unable to grant Moses' request. He does what he can. He hides his servant in a cleft in the rock and manifests his presence. But his face, his glory, is concealed from human eyes: 'I will put you in the cleft of the rock and cover you with my hand until I have passed by. Then I will take my hand away and you shall see my back, but my face shall not be seen' (Exod. 33:22,23). No man can look upon God because he is holy. Even the cherubim in Isaiah's temple vision veiled their eyes in the presence of God. If the sinless angelic beings which serve him ceaselessly must hide their faces, then how much more must we who are both mortal and sinful!

So God is invisible first of all because he is spirit, and secondly because he is holy. But there is a third reason why God should be described as 'invisible', namely because he is inscrutable by nature. 'My thoughts are not your thoughts, neither are your ways my ways,' says the Lord (Isa. 55:8). God's thoughts, plans and intentions are beyond our ken. Nobody knows the thoughts in the mind of God. Paul tells us in 1 Corinthians 2:11 that it is only the Spirit of God who can search out the divine mind. It is an enormous privilege that the same Spirit reveals those things, in part, to the believing soul. But such revealing in no way changes the essential truth that the mind of God is inscrutable, unknowable and inaccessible to human search.

There may be other ways in which the invisibility of God is expressed and demonstrated in Scripture, but what has been said already is enough for us to see the main implication of this teaching. It is clear that if God is to be known to man, *he must declare himself*. This is a most important conclusion and one that is fundamental to our understanding of the person and work of Jesus Christ.

Christ, the image of God

It is the uniform teaching of the New Testament that God *has* declared himself, and has done so in the person of Christ. Many scriptures substantiate this claim. John begins his Gospel with a sublime statement of the deity of Christ, and goes on to say, 'No man has seen God at any time; Christ the only-begotten Son, who is in the bosom of the Father, he has explained him' (John 1:18 mg). In John 6:46 we read, 'Not that any man has seen the Father, except the one that is from God; he has seen the Father.' These and other scriptures are very clear in what they are saying. God reveals himself through, and only through, the Son. We might recall the conversation that Jesus had with his disciple Philip. The latter makes what seems to be a reasonable request (John 14:8). 'Lord, show us the Father,' he asks, 'and it is enough for us.' But the response is anything but predictable: 'Have I been so long with you, and yet you have not come to know me, Philip? He who has seen me has seen the Father; how do you say, "Show us the Father"?'

It is therefore in Christ that God makes himself known. It is in Christ that the invisible God, the God on whom we cannot gaze and into whose mind we cannot peer, the God whose nature we cannot explore, declares and reveals himself. Notice that it is not a revelation of his *purposes* that he makes in Christ, for that he can do through human agencies. It is a revelation of *himself*.

Further support for these ideas is to be found in Hebrews 1:3, where we read of Christ, 'He is the radiance of [God's] glory and the exact representation of his nature.' As the sun's rays convey to us the light and warmth of the luminary itself, so God's glory comes to us through Christ. And as the sun cannot be seen at all except by the reception of those rays, so God is invisible apart from Christ. Were God knowable outside of Christ, it would be unnecessary for Christ to be the exact representation of his nature. It is no surprise, therefore, that when Ezekiel had a vision of the sovereign God, he saw 'a figure with the appearance of a man' (Ezek. 1:26), while Isaiah's vision of the Deity also featured Christ (John 12:41).

Our discussion of the invisibility of God has led us directly to an explanation of the entire statement under consideration in Colossians 1. When Paul tells us that Christ is the 'image of the invisible God' he is saying that God is to be seen in Christ, and in him alone. An image is a likeness, a representation of the object portrayed. Clearly Paul is not thinking in terms of a physical image, for God is Spirit. No more did Christ intend his words to be taken in a physical sense when he spoke to Philip. Christ's bodily form, his human nature, would tell Philip absolutely nothing about God. It was in the character of Christ that the Father was to be discerned. As John testifies, 'We beheld his glory, glory as of the only begotten from the Father, full of grace and truth' (John 1:14). It was the grace and truth of the Saviour that revealed the character of God to the wondering disciples. It is thus in the nature and character of Christ that God stands revealed.

We can turn this around and state the converse. God does not make himself known except through Christ. He does not communicate himself to man without Christ. Outside of Christ there is no true knowledge of God. I would extend this statement beyond the realm of soteriology. It is true that there is salvation in no other name than that of Christ, and that God may only be known savingly through his Son. But we cannot limit Paul's teaching here to the question of salvation. The invisibility of God is absolute, extending to all his attributes and works. So also Christ is the image or revelation of God in all his aspects.

I am sure we would all agree that God manifests his saving grace only in Christ, for he alone is the mediator of the new covenant. But the context in Colossians 1 demands a wider interpretation. It extends this idea beyond the question of soteriology. For immediately Paul has told us that Christ is the image of the invisible God, he proceeds to consider Christ in his relationship to the whole cosmos. He does not at this point introduce the subject of salvation, though he comes to it later. Christ is first presented as the image of God in the context, not of salvation, but of creation! There is a great deal in this chapter about the church and the saving work of Christ, but the immediate setting of this statement is the origin and sustenance of the physical universe. The context demands, therefore, that the idea that God reveals himself in Christ be applied to creation as fully as to redemption.

Some objections

God therefore cannot be known truly, regarding all of his work and regarding all of his nature, except in and through Christ. Eliminate Christ and you have an essentially unknown God. I shall put a lot of weight on this conclusion presently, and it is only fair therefore that I should pause at this point to consider two possible objections to the claim that I am making.

First of all, it may be argued that God revealed himself in Old Testament revelation, long before Jesus Christ came on the scene of human history. Therefore, surely, he revealed himself without Christ in the Old Testament. Secondly, it might be objected that God stands revealed in the book of nature, that is, through the creation. This seems to be taught in such scriptures as Psalm 19 and Romans 1. Let us look at these objections in turn.

Does the Old Testament constitute a non-Christological

revelation of God? It might seem so, even from the passage quoted above in Hebrews 1, for this begins, 'God, after he spoke long ago to the fathers in the prophets in many portions and in many ways in these last days has spoken to us in his Son' (Heb. 1:1,2). Does this not mean that God revealed himself apart from Christ in Old Testament times?

My answer to this is negative. We must remember that, as Christians, we must always interpret the Old Testament by the New. We must never think of the two Testaments as distinct, as if they somehow present two different messages. In fact the purpose of the Hebrews introduction is to emphasize the continuity between the two Testaments rather than a contrast. The New Testament will not allow us to treat the Old Testament as a Christless revelation. The Lord Jesus himself emphasized this on the road to Emmaus, when he showed his disciples 'the things concerning himself in all the [Old Testament]' scriptures. On another occasion, he said of the law and prophets, 'It is these which bear witness of me.'

Even in relation to the creation story itself, we shall see that the New Testament insists, again and again, that Christ was the Creator. This makes it impossible for us to read the creation story in a way that ignores the role of Christ. We cannot read the Old Testament as if we had not grasped the New. There may in many cases be no explicit references to the Messiah, but as we read in the New Testament, the Old is always interpreted for us in Christological terms. Providing we read the Old Testament in the light of the New, the principle that God reveals himself only in Christ remains intact.

What of the passage in Hebrews, then? Clearly the writer is referring to the historical sequence of revelation and also, of course, to the increased clarity with which the man Christ Jesus made God known. God's fulness of purpose was not known until Christ came in the flesh, but that does not mean the Old Testament is a Christless revelation. Indeed, John tells us that the enthroned Jehovah of Isaiah's vision was none other than Christ (Isa. 6; John 12:41), while the many theophanies (appearances of God in human form) recorded in the Old Testament can only be reconciled with the ineffability and invisibility of God if these were appearances of the pre-incarnate Christ.

The second objection can be voiced in the question: 'Does not God reveal himself outside of Christ in nature?' Obviously we could turn to Romans 1:20,21: 'For since the creation of the world [God's] invisible attributes, his eternal power and divine nature, have been clearly seen, being understood through what has been made, so that they are without excuse. For even though they knew God, they did not honour him as God . . .'

We accept that God's glory, power and Godhead are discernible in nature, but we have to ask two questions. Firstly, is man capable of reading the book of nature? We can easily misunderstand these verses unless we read on to see how ancient man reacted to this revelation. What Romans 1 teaches is that man has turned his back upon this particular revelation. Because of sin, he is incapable of correctly reading the book of nature. God is indeed revealed in nature, (and in conscience also, as we read in Romans 2:15), and these revelations are such as to leave man without excuse for his atheism. Nevertheless man in his fallen state is incapable of recognizing God in his creation. This avenue of revelation is closed to man because of his fallen nature.

Man cannot say, 'I had no means of knowing about God,' but his blindess to general revelation is both total and culpable. He is dead in trespasses and sins. He is dead, being incapable of responding to the stimuli which are there, but he is dead *in sins*. That is, his incapacity is not a misfortune for which he bears no responsibility, but is rather a state for which God holds him fully responsible.

This surely is the import of what Paul writes in Romans 1. The passage starts in 1:18 where we read, 'The wrath of God is revealed against all ungodliness and unrighteousness of men, who suppress the truth in unrighteousness.' We are left in no doubt that man is guilty for ignoring his Creator. At the same time, man's 'foolish heart was darkened', that is, man is blind to spiritual realities. As Paul writes elsewhere, 'A natural man does not accept the things of the Spirit of God, for they are foolishness to him, and he cannot understand them because they are spiritually appraised' (1 Cor. 2:14). I do not think Romans 1 is saying that ancient man was once able to perceive God in creation but became progressively blind to him. The sequence recorded by the apostle is surely a logical progression that applies to men of all generations, rather than a historical progression that divides the ancients from ourselves. The logical progression sees unrighteousness as the precursor and cause of spiritual blindness, not the reverse. That is why man remains guilty in his blindness, rather than being an object of pity in the eyes of God.

Although therefore it is true that God is the Author of the book
of nature, and although it is true that certain of God's characteristics are revealed in nature, it is still true that man can only know
this invisible God through Christ. The book of nature is closed to
the eyes of the natural man. He may indeed deduce from nature a
belief in a god or gods, but what he sees will bear no resemblance
to the true God. A modern example of this is afforded by the astronomers Hoyle and Wickramasinghe in their book *Evolution from
Space*, mentioned in the previous chapter. By examining the structure of living molecules they come to the conclusion that life could
not have evolved without the intervention of intelligent beings.
Thus they entitle their final chapter 'Convergence to God'. But
they are at pains to point out that their 'god' is not to be confused
with the God of the Bible or, indeed, the gods of any traditional religion. They remain blind, therefore, to the true being and nature
of God, in spite of their 'creationist' insights. It is in Christ, and in
Christ alone, that the invisible God effectually reveals himself to
man.

If this is the case, if God can be truly known only in Christ,
where does this leave our various theories of origins?

Theories of origins

Any theory of origins that bypasses Christ, whether evolutionary
or creationist, must inevitably lead us to false conclusions. That is
the thesis that I am advancing in this chapter. Whether we are
considering atheistical evolution, which obviously leaves Christ
out, or theistic evolution, which has a place for God or at least for
a deity, but has no Christological content, or whether we are talk-
ing about scientific creationism divorced from Scripture – in all of
these cases the theory of origins is bound to be defective since the
essential role of Christ is excluded from consideration. (Obviously
a Christological content can be superimposed upon theistic evolution and scientific creationism, but it is not of the essence of these
theories and is therefore superfluous to them.)

Let us pause for a moment with the subject of scientific
creationism. I do not want to be misunderstood and I must therefore define my terms carefully. Scientific creationism is legitimate
if by that term we mean the reconciliation of scientific obser-

vations with biblical revelation. In other words, if all we are doing in scientific creationism is to examine the findings or data of science and demonstrate that they are consistent with biblical revelation, then that is perfectly proper. However, if by scientific creationism we mean an attempt to discover the fact of creation, the nature of the Creator or the purpose of the created order by scientific investigation, unaided by biblical revelation, then I fear that we are in serious danger.

Many readers will be familiar with the situation in the U.S.A., which has been the seed-bed of creationism in recent years. Because religious teaching is not permitted in the public school system, some creationists have tried to promote scientific creationism as opposed to revelatory or biblical creationism. Setting aside the biblical revelation, Christian theology or Christian belief, they arrive at the conclusion that the cosmos was created and did not evolve, simply by examining the natural world. This is the version of scientific creationism against which I am arguing. It is quite clear that Jehovah's Witnesses can subscribe to this form of creationism. So can Buddhists and atheists.

Let me return to the example of the astronomers Hoyle and Wickramasinghe, who have arrived at the conclusion that life could not possibly have evolved by chance. It is necessary therefore in their opinion to posit an intelligent creator or originator of life. They have arrived at that position purely by intellectual argument and scientific reasoning. They are not Christians. They are 'scientific creationists' in the sense that their logic and their scientific enquiries have led them to the conclusion that only intelligence could have brought life into being. This form of scientific creationism is not only ascriptural, but is actually anti-scriptural. For if Scripture is telling us that the creator God can only be known through Christ, then any attempt to understand creation which bypasses biblical revelation is doomed to failure.

I hope I have made the distinction clear between two things that can be described as scientific creationism. The one claims that the biblical revelation is authoritative and seeks to demonstrate that scientific observations of the universe are consistent with that revelation. The other sets out quite deliberately to bypass revelation and to prove creation as opposed to evolution on the grounds of scientific evidence alone. That to me is not only a-biblical but anti-biblical.

This, I think, is why the New Testament places such tremendous emphasis upon the fact that Christ is the Creator. Again and again, as we go from John 1 to Colossians 1 to Hebrews 1, we find this insistence that Christ created all things. It is not sufficient in the eyes of the New Testament writers to say that God is the Creator. It has to be Christ. In the prologue to his Gospel, the apostle John goes out of his way to impose a Christology on Genesis 1. He borrows its phraseology: 'In the beginning was the Word.' Compare that with the oft-repeated statement, 'God said,' in Genesis. He tells us that Christ was 'in the beginning with God' and that 'All things came into being through him.' Just as in Genesis God sent light upon earth, so Christ was 'the true light which ... enlightens every man' (John 1:1–9).

It seems to me that the New Testament insistence upon a Christocentric creationism is not accidental, an unnecessary gloss on the story of creation. Rather, it is fundamental to the message of the apostles and there is no clearer demonstration of this fact than the very passage before us in Colossians 1.

Christ and the cosmos

We have considered at some length the relationship of Christ to God. We must now move on, with the apostle, to think of the relationship of Christ to the cosmos. We read, 'He is the first-born of all creation.' This particular statement is sometimes used by unitarians to argue that Christ is part of the created order. He is, they claim, the first-born in the sense of the first created being, through whom God then proceeded to work out the remainder of the creation. But this is a blatant misinterpretation and is ruled out of court by the very words that follow at the beginning of verse 16: 'For in him all things were created.' Christ cannot be both the Creator of 'all things' and part of that creation. If he is the Creator of all things, he must necessarily stand outside of the created order.

An even stronger argument to disarm this particular error is to be found in the word 'first-born'. If we turn to the first chapter of Hebrews we find that the distinction is emphasized between Christ, who is 'born', and the angelic orders, who are created. 'To which of the angels did [God] ever say, "Thou art my Son, today I have begotten thee"?' (Heb. 1:5.) The argument is that Christ is not created. He is not the work of God's hands but, rather, God's progeny. This, is, of course, an anthropomorphism, but the essence of human generation is the fact that the progeny share the nature and characteristics of the parents. This is the whole force of the idea of begetting. He, says John, is the 'only begotten', the one who solely and uniquely shares the attributes of God. Therefore the idea that 'first-begotten' suggests in some way that Christ is part of the creation (albeit the first to be created), is ruled out by the very word itself.

Nor can it be argued that if Christ is the first-begotten, there must have been others, begotten subsequently, who are like him, therefore he is not unique and cannot be God. For the word 'first-born' may denote pre-eminence rather than chronology. Priority can denote priority in time, the first-born being simply the first child born into a family, or it can signify rank. We can describe the heir to a throne as the first-born in the land even though there are many older than he. The term describes both the blood relationship of the first-born to the sovereign and his rank as the heir to his father's throne. There is therefore no necessary implication that there are others like the first-born. The first child in a family remains the first-born even if he or she is an only child!

So priority can refer to time or to rank. Fortunately we do not need to debate which is intended in verse 17 because both are found here. Priority in time is, of course, to be understood as priority before time began. 'He is [existed] before all things.' To the Jews who criticized him, Jesus said, 'Before Abraham was, I am.' He took to himself the ineffable and eternal name of God, the 'I AM', the one who stands outside of time, who is the same 'yesterday, today and for ever', as Hebrews tells us of Christ. He is therefore prior in time, the eternal self-existent God, with whom there is neither past nor future, for all is present.

His priority in rank tells us even more about Christ and the cosmos than does his priority in time. First of all, Colossians informs us, he is the Creator. We have already seen that the New Testament always ascribes the work of creation to Christ. 'In him all things were created . . . all things have been created through him and for him' (Col. 1:16).

The biblical writers use several different prepositions in this context. In Hebrews 1, for example, both the Father and the Son are mentioned in relation to creation: 'God has spoken to us *in* his Son . . . *through* whom also he made the world.' Here in Colossians 1:16 two prepositions are used: '*In* him all things were created' and, at the end of the verse, 'All things have been created *through* him.' The way prepositions are translated often depends on the version consulted. The Authorized Version, for example, says 'By him were all things created.' I think, however, that the NASV is as close to the original as any in using the words 'in' and 'through'.

What does Paul mean? Does he mean that God the Father created the universe by using Christ as his agent? Is this a reference to the agency of Christ in creation when we read, 'All things have been created through him'? I think not. The idea that Christ is the agent of creation is a weaker concept than that which the Bible actually proposes to us. It is a concept that Paul himself had to be careful to avoid in the Colossian context, for one of the problems that Paul had to combat at Colosse was the Gnostic heresy. According to this teaching, Christ was just one of a large succession of spiritual beings, of different ranks and orders, linking the unholy, impure physical world with the remote purity of the spiritual realm. To some extent this is what the Jehovah's Witnesses teach today, that Christ is the great intermediary between God and man, but is himself not equal to God.

We have to understand that Paul had consciously to avoid any hint of Gnosticism as he wrote to Colosse. It seems to me therefore that he must be using these two prepositions quite deliberately and with great care.

Although Paul says all things were created 'through Christ', as if speaking of an intermediary or agent, he begins the verse with a different preposition: 'In him all things were created.' This is important. You cannot say of an agent that things were done *in* him. You may say they were done 'through' him, but the word 'in' is not appropriate to an agent. Rather, it implies that the person described is an essential part of the whole picture. We could perhaps paraphrase the meaning thus: 'All things were created in relationship to Christ', or 'with regard to Christ', or 'with reference' to him. We are not to understand the role of Christ as that of an intermediary through whom creation took place, but rather as the creative self-expression of God. That is, the Father's creative will, which brought the entire cosmos into existence, was being expressed in Christ.

Perhaps the easy way to get this across is to say that, just as God was in Christ reconciling the world to himself, so he was in Christ calling that world into being. Christ was not simply an agent through whom God performed this task, but God was in Christ creating the cosmos.

So then we have this priority in rank expressed in the fact that Christ was the Creator. It is of great significance that John calls Christ 'the Word' and links this with the creative activity of God. The expression 'God said . . .' employed in Genesis was not merely a dramatic device or figure of speech. It has special significance in relation to the fact that Christ is the Logos, the Word of God. God's creative acts were brought about by words, the putting forth of the will and mind of God. Words are vehicles of self-expression and the creation was nothing less than that – an expression of the will of God and, in part, a discovery of his nature. Christ may be the Word of God in other senses, but he is the Word first in this creative context.

Not only is Christ the Creator, however, but he is the Creator of all. We do not need to spend a great deal of time upon this, but we should notice the emphasis placed upon this claim in verse 16. In fact most of this verse is written to establish the comprehensive character of the creative work of Christ. 'In him all things were created, both in the heavens and on earth, visible and invisible, whether thrones or dominions or rulers or authorities . . . all things have been created through him and for him.'

John places a similar emphasis on the totality of Christ's work, repeating the assertion both positively and negatively ('All things came into being through him; and apart from him nothing came into being that has come into being,' John 1:3). We might ask why there should be this insistence on the comprehensiveness of the creative work of Christ. Surely it is to combat the Gnostic error, in which Christ might be put on the same level as other spiritual dignitaries. If he is the Creator of all, then he stands uniquely above all creation in rank.

This is brought out particularly by the reference to 'thrones, dominions, rulers and authorities'. There is a debate between creationists and theistic evolutionists over the meaning of these terms. The theistic evolutionist does not draw any distinction between creation and providence, since in his view creation was accomplished by providential means rather than by miracle. If by thrones and dominions etc., Paul means the human institutions of history, controlled by the sovereignty of God (Dan. 4:32), then there is no distinction in the verse between Christ creating 'all things' and his providential rule 'over the realm of mankind'.

On the other hand, there is a difference in tense between the act of creation described in verse 16 (they were created) and the sustaining work of providence mentioned in verse 17 ('In him all things *hold* together'). Creation would thus appear to be a finished work lying in the past, while providence remains an ongoing reality. This, of course, is wholly consistent with Genesis 2:1–3, where creation is described as fully complete.

In fact, Paul is almost certainly not speaking of human institutions at all in verse 16. There is no reason for him to pick out these human institutions for special mention. Remember he is seeking to combat a heresy which had erected a whole system of *spiritual* authorities and intermediaries, angelic powers, between God and man, and it is those powers and thrones that Paul here subjects to Christ. Whatever spiritual powers there may be, he says, were created by Christ and therefore cannot be considered superior or even equal to him. Paul does not deny the existence of spiritual powers. He refers to them on various occasions, notably in Ephesians 3:10 and 6:12 ('rulers and the authorities in the heavenly places'). But what he does insist is that Christ is always superior to them (Heb. 1:4).

It seems to me that the apostle is simply using human analogies and terms of sovereignty and rule to describe the angelic powers with which alone he is concerned in this part of the epistle (see e.g. 1:13; 2:8 –10; 2:15 –18).

So Christ is the Creator of all things, but that is not all. His priority is further demonstrated by the fact that he is the Sustainer of the cosmos ('In him all things hold together,' v.17). That is to say, all things derive their integrity from the very existence and will of Christ. The same truth is taught in Hebrews 1:3, where we read that he 'upholds all things by the word of his power'.

A final and most important point arises in our discussion of Christ's priority in rank. We are told in verse 16 that all things were created 'for' him. It seems to me that here we have a clear statement of the very purpose of the cosmos. All things were created not only in Christ, not only through Christ, but also *for* him. That is to say, it is the intention of God that the cosmos should subserve the glory and fulfilment of Christ. The cosmos can be seen as an arena in which the glory of Christ is demonstrated, in which the purposes of Christ are worked out and in which the will, mind and character of Christ can be expressed. That, according to the apostle, is the purpose of the cosmos.

This is a most important idea. We usually think of the cosmos as just being 'there', as if it were simply part of a deistic scheme of things. Then, quite separately, we think of Jesus Christ coming to earth for the purpose of saving sinners. The latter, of course, is perfectly correct, but the New Testament does not present things in quite this way. There are few chapters of the Bible that say as much about the saving work of Christ as does Colossians 1. Read verses 13,14 and 20–23. But it is this very subject of salvation that leads Paul to introduce the cosmic role of Christ. He sees the cross of Christ as the place where God was reconciling not only sinners but *all things* to himself (v.20), whether on earth or in heaven. If the work of Christ is to carry this wider significance, then Christ himself must be seen as the Creator and Sustainer of the cosmos. No smaller view of him is admissible if he is to be the Reconciler of all things. No lesser view properly represents the saving work of Christ in all its fulness and cosmic implication.

Christ and the church

We now turn to our final topic, the relationship of Christ to the church. Clearly we could examine this relationship at great length, exploring it in many ways, in many figures and in many great doctrines. That, however, is not my purpose here. What I want to point out is the way his relationship to the church is linked with his relationship to the cosmos. Looking at our passage, we see there is no real pause between verses 17 and 18. 'He is before all things, and in him all things hold together. He is also head of the body, the church.' There is no change of 'gear' at this point. The argument flows smoothly from one verse to the next. Paul's theme is the pre-eminence of Christ in *all* realms, whether church, cosmos or heaven.

If we look back to Ephesians 1:22,23 we find an even more striking example of the way Paul relates Christ's cosmic role to his headship of the church. It is a brief statement that can easily be missed. We read, God has 'put all things in subjection under his feet, and gave him as head over all things to the church, which is his body, the fulness of him who fills all in all'. Notice that he is not just Head over all things (the cosmic Christ). Nor is he simply Head over the church (the Saviour), but Head over all things *to* the church.

What does that mean? Let us express it in this way: Christ is Head over all things *for the sake of the church*. His dominance and priority over the created order is for the sake or benefit of the church. Of course, the converse is true, that the church exists for the sake and glory of Christ, since we have already seen that the whole of creation is 'for' him. But it is equally true that creation is not just for the benefit of Christ in a vague and general sense. Creation is for Christ *through* the church and this leads us to the sobering thought that the church of Jesus Christ is really the *raison d'être* of creation. The cosmos exists in order that the church might exist!

In case this seems to be a rather extreme statement, let us consider further what Paul is saying in Ephesians 1:23. 'The church, which is his body, [is] the fulness of him who fills all in all.' Now that is a staggering claim. The church (that is, the glorified church) is the fulness of Christ. Christ is fulfilled in the church.

How can this be? How can any created entity fulfil Christ? How can God become in any way more complete or perfect? At first sight the idea seems inadmissible, for it implies that the perfection of God is somehow incomplete without the church. Surely he is perfect to begin with? Yet the New Testament teaches clearly that, somehow, Christ *is* fulfilled in the church, for the church is the fulness of him who fills all in all.

Perhaps we can glimpse an understanding of what all this means by using another great New Testament picture of the church, namely that it is the bride of Christ. Human marriage at its best is recognized as the fulfilment of the desires and personalities of the partners involved. The taking of a bride fulfils the manhood of a human husband, for marriage is a completion of the human state, an element of human destiny. If marriage can be regarded as the consummation of manhood and womanhood, then by analogy we can see how Christ's union with the church can be described as his 'fulness'. The uniting of human partners fulfils certain potentialities, certain possibilities which are present but dormant until the marriage is established and consummated. Thus we can see how the church may be the fulness of Christ since it fulfils his potential for love, grace, mercy and saving power, characteristics of the Godhead that would remain for ever unexpressed without the church.

Here, then, we have the element that completes Paul's unifying picture of Christ and the cosmos. The universe was created for Christ, not only in a general sense but specifically that the church might come into being. As the bride of Christ, that glorified church represents the culmination of God's ultimate purpose, 'the summing up of all things in Christ' (Eph. 1:10).

Conclusion

There are, of course, many other passages of Scripture, full of significance for the matters we have been studying, which we have not space to discuss. There is even much in Colossians 1 that we have not considered and which would further illuminate the subject of Christ and the cosmos. What has been said, however, should help us to see how important it is to have a Christological view of creation. Mere creationism, or even scientific creationism, can never be enough. Nor is it sufficient that such creationism is held and promoted by Bible-believing Christians. We must insist that a right emphasis be placed on the Christology of creation whenever we approach this and related subjects such as miracles, providence and eschatology.

References

1. F. Hoyle and N.C. Wickramasinghe, *Evolution from Space*, J.M. Dent & Sons Ltd, 1981.